The Dreams of Two *Yi-min*

The Dreams
of Two *Yi-min*

Margaret K. Pai

A Kolowalu Book
UNIVERSITY OF HAWAII PRESS • HONOLULU

Manufactured in the United States of America

94 93 92 91 90 89   5 4 3 2 1

Library of Congress Cataloging-in-Publication Data
Pai, Margaret K., 1914–
    The dreams of two yi-min / Margaret K. Pai.
        p.   cm. — (A Kolowalu book)
    Includes index.
    ISBN 0–8248–1179–8 :
    1. Pai, Margaret K., 1914–   . 2. Korean Americans—Hawaii-
-Biography. 3. Hawaii—Social life and customs. 4. Hawaii-
-Economic conditions—1918–1959. 5. Immigrants—Hawaii-
-History—20th century. I. Title.
DU624.7.K67P34 1989
996.9'004957024—dc19
    [B]
                                                           88–29539
                                                              CIP

    The paper used in this publication meets the
minimum requirements of American National Stan-
dard for Information Sciences—Permanence of
Paper for Printed Library Materials
                            ANSI Z39.48-1984

To Merphil and Garet

Contents

Preface

I often look back with a special fondness to a certain vivid period in my childhood—to the years when our family lived in a small fenced-in complex of old, dilapidated buildings in Honolulu. There my father struggled as an immigrant entrepreneur engaged in the only trade he had learned—furniture upholstering; my mother worked alongside him; and my sister, two brothers, and I grew up amidst the factory noises, paint fumes, and dust.

Living there in the 1930s my parents faced the threat of financial doom every day. Their sheer will to survive kept our family unusually close; although we children had no perception of the business world, we were continually aware of the precarious life we led, as if we were in a small boat all alone out in a stormy sea. My father's ingenuity brought him a small measure of success, yet we were very, very poor by any standard during those Depression days.

Gradually in my memories the factory noises, smells, and dust cast a haze of nostalgia, and I felt I must recount the period that once seemed so threatening and fearful. I wrote the article "Growing Up in a Factory," which was published in *Honolulu* Magazine in November 1978. Subsequently, numerous requests from readers, friends, and family members for more information about my parents led me to write this book.

I could not begin the story of my parents without telling how they met: my mother emigrated from Korea to be the bride of a man she picked from a handful of pictures. This would serve as a good "once upon a time" beginning for their story, I thought. However, I realized I had to begin even earlier and tell that my father had come to the Hawaiian Islands as a very young contract sugar plantation worker.

Before long I found I could not ignore the historical frame of my mother's and father's dreams. Thus I have included the drama of Korean politics in the immigrant community in Hawaii at the beginning of the twentieth century, which brought the narrative to focus on the pivotal roles played by the Methodist church, the Korean Independence Movement, and Syngman Rhee. We children mistakenly thought then that our parents were squabbling over petty politics. But the repercussions of the political upheaval in that period in the Korean community continued long into the decades that followed and are still felt to this day.

My father was often called a man with strange ideas, and my mother and her children accepted the notion that he was indeed odd. He continually tried to give shape to his ideas in the form of patents. One of my proudest moments was when I made the trip many years later to the U.S. Patent and Trademark Office in Crystal City, Virginia, just outside of Washington, D.C., where pictures of Thomas Edison, Henry Ford, Alexander Graham Bell, and other inventors hang in the entry hall. In the library inside I found my father's patents on file and I was able to make copies of the diagrams of his seven patents.

This book tells of the day-to-day activities of our family and the families we knew—from 1914, when I was born, through the Great Depression, World War II, and the postwar years, to the middle of this century.

All her life my mother revered education. In this book I touch briefly on the school system in Hawaii in the early years. There was an unevenness in the kind of education available to a child: it made a difference whether the child lived in an urban or rural area or whether he or she could speak Standard English. In some instances, being female closed the doors of learning to a youngster.

In my father's quest for the good life, his business brought him into contact with the rich, the famous, and the well-educated, some of whom were cunning and, perhaps, malevolent.

To a man who had received only a high school education in a country school in his homeland, my father certainly lacked the sophistication that a college education might have afforded him; he also lacked the English skills to deal with these people, many of whom had money and power.

Yet with the aid of my mother's keen perception of people and circumstances, my parents rose from the poverty of the sugar plantation laborer to realize many of their dreams in the new world.

I am indebted to several of my literary friends who were involved with me in this book from beginning to end. One of them especially, Catherine Harris, had the vision and faith to urge me to start it; Shirley Sanders, Barbara Robinson, Nancy Mower, and Jane Gubelin patiently waited for each new chapter. I am also indebted to the Hawaii Writers Club for their encouragement and their criticism of the pages I read to them. My thanks to Georgine Fong and Shirley Sanders for typing parts of the manuscript before I got a word processor.

I am particularly grateful to Dr. Yong-ho Choe, Professor of Korean History at the University of Hawaii, who read through my manuscript and offered valuable suggestions on how to clarify historical and language factors, identify certain geographical places, and correct the use of Korean verbs. To Dr. Dong Jay Lee, Professor of Korean Language at the University of Hawaii, I am grateful for his review of the spelling and definitions of the Korean words I use in the text.

Esther Arinaga thoughtfully read through the manuscript and pointed out where more details could be added to certain events she remembered well about our family, and the Rev. Nelson Kwon added to my recollection of some of the activities of GIs during World War II.

To Dr. Alice Chai, Kam Pui Lai, and Violet Lai I owe much for their words of encouragement and for their sharing of ideas on Asian culture. To Young Ok Kang and Irving Rosen I wish to give credit for reproducing several old, rare photographs of people and places in Hawaii in the early 1900s.

I appreciate the invitation of Mrs. Chung Song Ahn to meet and interview her guest, the venerable ninety-year-old Tough Chin Ho, who was a revolutionary in Korea during the terrible 1919 demonstration when the Japanese occupied their homeland. Fortunately, I was able to catch him between planes on one of his frequent trips from Korea and the mainland United States.

And finally my thanks to my editors: Damaris Kirchhofer, for her patience and suggestions for the manuscript in the early stages, and to Jean Brady, for her invaluable help and critical assistance in following the manuscript to its publication.

In the text, when naming persons living in Korea I have used the Korean system of last names followed by their first names, and when naming persons living outside of Korea, as in Hawaii, I have used the American system of first names followed by last.

The Dreams of Two *Yi-min*

CHAPTER I

The New World

ONE day in Taegu, Korea, a man with a large packet of pictures, acting as a go-between, called on the Lee Cho Sung family. The year was 1912. In the beautifully furnished sitting room, with bronze-trimmed chests and scenic scrolls on the walls, he informed them that he knew of an unparalleled opportunity for their daughters to become rich if they married bachelors living in Hawaii. He painted glowing pictures of how prosperous these men were and how they moved in circles with other wealthy men of position and prestige.

The Lees had two daughters of marriageable age. One was twenty, the other eighteen. Both girls were demurely seated on the matted floor with their bright silk skirts spread around them, their faces alert, their dark hair sleekly combed.

The go-between handed the photos to the girls' parents, who glanced over the pictures, then passed them to their daughters. The older daughter kept very quiet. The younger, Hee Kyung, surprised the go-between when she asked, "Is there a college I can attend if I should go to Hawaii?"

"Yes, I'm certain there is," came his quick reply.

Shy and timid, the older girl slowly went over the pictures. She thought how work-worn the men looked. She gradually drew back from the photos, as if each man was giving her a fiercer look than the last. She shook her head.

The younger daughter, however, took the pictures eagerly and carefully studied the faces. Each portrait, measuring three by two-and-a-half inches, showed only a man's head and shoulders. She lingered over one—was it his large, dark eyes or his resolute chin that attracted her?

The go-between noticed her returning again and again to the same picture. He moved to where she sat and read the inscription on the back of the picture. "This man's name is Kwon Do In," he said. "He lives in Honolulu."

Hee Kyung softly repeated, "Kwon Do In, Kwon Do In."

"You may have the picture," the go-between offered as he gathered up the rest of the photos. "I hope you will decide to be a *yi-min*." He spoke briefly on departure procedures and mentioned the dates when other brides would be leaving for the new world. Then he moved on to lure more brides.

My mother, Hee Kyung Lee, sailed into Honolulu Harbor one October morning in 1912 as an eighteen-year-old picture bride. Looking radiant in her pink *cho-gori* and *chi-ma,* her thick, black hair braided in a crown, she saw the man whose picture she held in her hand. She noted her husband-to-be also held a picture. He was thin but he looked strong. His black hair was short, his eyes dark and round.

They were led to the Immigration Station nearby. As she walked beside him, her heart fluttered at the thought of a new life in a new land with the man she had just met. They joined other Korean brides, who had come with her on the same ship, and their Hawaii grooms. A clergyman came and married all the couples.

Kwon piled his wife's bags and boxes in a hand-drawn cart. Pushing it, he made his way with his wife from the harbor to their home on Punchbowl Street.

The moment the bride stepped into her new home she was overcome with dismay. Only one room to cook and sleep and entertain in. The bare wooden floor. Sparse, crude furnishings. Even the servants' quarters in her home back in Taegu looked better. She was like a flower rudely transplanted in foreign soil. How had she come to choose this harsh life? For many days she cried when alone. Her life was nothing like what she had imagined or what her parents wanted for her.

Before long she became aware of her husband's meager wages. She knew she had to abandon her dream of attending college in Hawaii.

My father, Do In Kwon, was twenty-four when his wife arrived. He worked as a yardboy in the Manoa Valley for H. Hackfeld, a prominent businessman. The wages were so low that after some months had passed he asked his boss if he could rent and farm a piece of land adjacent to his property. When asked what he would do with the land, Kwon replied, "I like grow vegetables. I like sell. Make extra money." Hackfeld consented. When the young farmer produced enough to fill a cart he made his way on foot with the cart all the way from Manoa to the busy fish and vegetable vendors on River Street. Only a few days before he met his wife Kwon had hurriedly rented a shabby one-room apartment. He had not wished to show her his mean living quarters behind his employer's mansion.

Kwon confided to his wife that he hoped for a better life. Ironically, at present he was doing the very kind of work he had tried to escape in Korea. He began, "After I graduated from high school in Andong, I had no means to go to college. You know, Andong is a small country town. Only one boy in my school got a scholarship to a college in Tokyo; he scored the highest in an exam. I was only the second highest. I was so disappointed. I had nothing to look forward to but farming with my father."

"So what did you do?" Hee Kyung asked. For the first time she was aware that her husband prized education.

"Then I heard about Hawaii. The sugar plantations were looking for laborers from Korea. I applied. I was rejected immediately because I was underage. I was only seventeen then. But I persisted. Finally I got to board the SS *Siberia* bound for Hawaii, and left my parents and brothers behind. The ship docked in Honolulu Harbor on 13 February 1905."

A few months later Kwon mentioned that in June of the same year he had reached Hawaii, Japan abruptly cut off the flow of

Korean labor emigration because it was feared that Korean laborers would undermine the predominant position of the Japanese labor force in the Hawaiian market. Japan also resented the sugar planters' reluctance to import more Japanese workers. Korea was not annexed to Japan until 1910, but in 1905 Japan already exerted enormous power and control in the country.

His wife said, "You were lucky to escape before Japan took over our country. Now Japanese soldiers are everywhere. There are so many rules we must obey."

Despite that she found freedom from Japanese oppression in Hawaii, it was one dreary day after another for Hee Kyung. She tried to find something useful and interesting to do each day. But Sunday was the special day that she looked forward to. Her husband took her to worship at the Korean Methodist Church. She put on her prettiest *cho-gori* and *chi-ma,* and he wore his only suit. They walked down Punchbowl Street to the sanctuary, which filled with over a hundred men and women. She mingled happily with other picture brides who wore their colorful native dress. Like her new friends, she found immense comfort and solace in the Methodist church. She believed her religion survived well the transplanting process.

Before leaving Korea, Hee Kyung had been in close contact with the missionaries of the Methodist church in Taegu, who were affiliated with the Methodist Hawaiian Board of Missions in Honolulu. Her compatriots too had been Christians in their homeland. They all found inspiration in the Christian teachings. The missionaries had told them about their own ancestors who fled to America because of unbearable religious and political tyranny in their countries. They urged Koreans to travel to Hawaii to better their political and economic life, and to find much opportunity to convert people to Christianity by spreading the word of God.

The church in Honolulu offered all the social, political, and religious life the Kwons needed. It was easy for them to be assimilated into the large community. The members spoke the same language, felt the same pangs of political loss, and shared their knowledge, hopes, and dreams.

Hee Kyung realized that there was neither the time nor the money to pursue higher education. The urgent task for her was to learn to cook and sew. Above all, she had to learn to make good kim chee—a daily staple in every Korean home—that peppery cabbage that gave zest to a meal. Her husband said he had waited a long time for a wife who would make him good kim chee. How chagrined she was that she failed at the task so many times. She found that making this dish was an art. Her poor husband put up alternately with the bland, the oversalty, the sour, and the bitter results of her efforts without complaint. Some of her women friends made superb, delicious kim chee. She tried to do as they did but success for her was only occasional. How she regretted she had not learned to cook earlier in her life.

She compared notes with other picture brides. What brought them to the shores of the new world? Their stories were pitiful and poignant. Some were downright funny. One lady recounted a little shamefacedly, "This man told me to expect to see money growing on every tree. My eyes were dreamy. I believed him because he said everybody in Hawaii was rich. When I got here and saw only a few dried-up trees I thought I was a fool."

Another lady said, "I was already married to a man younger than myself. We were not poor. But my husband had a concubine and he spent every night out drinking. So I decided to run away. My parents were angry. When I came to Hawaii the man waiting for me was so old and poor—he was forty years old and working on the plantation. I had to work like a servant."

Still another lady related, "The go-between said there would be so much food we'd never be hungry. That stuck in my mind. On the farm there was never enough to eat. Look at me now. My husband doesn't earn enough so I have to scrimp and save. I have to take in washing and ironing for unmarried men. And a baby keeps coming every year!"

Soon after his bride's arrival, Kwon told her about the years he had spent on the sugar plantation. "After I landed in Honolulu, many of the men who had come on the *Siberia* with me were shipped to Koloa, which is on the island of Kauai. We worked hard. I got paid only sixteen dollars a month because I was so young. The other men got eighteen dollars."

"How long did you stay on the plantation?" Hee Kyung asked.

"Four long years. We didn't like the work. The hours were long and the work was hard. We heard there were better-paying jobs in Honolulu. We imagined Honolulu was a big, glamorous metropolis. When we first came to Hawaii as *yi-min,* we all dreamed of wealth."

Kwon stopped for a moment and looked pensive. Then he added, "We could see no way of getting rich if we remained on Kauai. So we took the boat to the big city. Honolulu was a busy city. There was much to see. But we had to find work."

The young bride listened sympathetically.

"Somehow I heard about a job as a yardboy. I grabbed it. My boss was Mr. Hackfeld. I was twenty-one then. My friends got other kinds of jobs, as houseboys or as laundry shop helpers. We all earned so little. I began farming vegetables on the side after my work on my boss' yard.

"Then we heard of men who were getting wives from Korea. We were excited. We thought we should wait till we saved enough money. When we heard that it might take months or years before we could get a wife we started our application. First, we wore our Sunday suits and went to a photo studio.

"I trembled when I handed my picture to an agent. Some of the men were so nervous they laughed, as if the whole thing was a joke. One man asked, 'If my wife is fat and ugly can I send her back?' The agent glared at him. He scolded, 'Our work is very serious.' We didn't know whether he meant no fat girls would be sent."

Korean men and women did not socialize together. The women met for pleasure in a social club or to help each other. Men met to discuss politics or to play cards.

In one of the men's social groups Kwon became acquainted with a man named Sung Moo Lee, who was a trainee refinisher in a furniture store. Kwon was envious of Lee's luck in finding such a respectable job. One day this friend informed Kwon there was an opening for an apprentice upholsterer in his firm, Coyne Furniture Company. Although he did not know what an upholsterer did, Kwon jumped at the opportunity and left Hackfeld's employ.

Two years after she came to the new world Hee Kyung gave birth to her first child. She and her husband named her Chung Sook, meaning "straight and upright" and "clear and gentle like a brook." I was that daughter.

Although my father enjoyed learning his craft at the furniture shop, the wages he brought home still barely covered the necessities of life.

Home, church, and a society called the Youngnam Puin Hoe made up my mother's whole world. At her church she helped form the Methodist Ladies Aid Society, a powerful organization that provided a network of services reaching every Korean family in the community. Although the immigrants were all poor, so dedicated were the Society members that no family went without food or a roof over their heads (immigrant men often lost their jobs); a mother who became ill could depend on other mothers to help her; and a mother with a newborn baby did not have to rise from her bed until she was strong. All these services were rendered despite the fact that every woman was burdened with heavy responsibilities of her own.

The Youngnam Puin Hoe was a society that a good number of the immigrant women belonged to. The members were *yi-min*, from a province in Korea called Kyungsangdo. These lively, bright-eyed ladies laughed easily and talked incessantly when they got together. They met once a month on Sunday afternoons (they observed the Sabbath by attending church and by not working that day). They helped the poor and the sick as an extension of the Methodist Society's work but looked for other projects as well.

A project that captured their fancy and enthusiasm soon appeared. The desire for freedom of their country from Japanese rule was always in their hearts. They spoke often of possible ways Koreans could win liberty, and of hopes for Japan's ultimate destruction. One day they heard a rumor from Los Angeles that spread to Hawaii, Shanghai, Manchuria—wherever Koreans lived.

It was a plan for a massive demonstration in Korea that would bring freedom and relief from Japan's rule. The purpose of the demonstration was to show the imperialists of Japan that Koreans were a strong, unified people, not the weaklings the oppressors made them appear to be. The public expression would attract the world's attention and cause nations to come to the rescue of Koreans suffering from oppression and humiliation.

Month after month as new details of the plan were received by the Youngnam Puin Hoe, the members' interest grew. The women declared they would go to Korea and participate in the demonstration.

However, it wasn't long before their enthusiasm diminished and their group plans collapsed when they realized they lacked the funds to cover the boat fare. Furthermore, who would care for their husbands and babies while they were gone?

My mother begged her friends to find a way to Korea and persisted in fanning the fire of fighting for freedom. She told them of the disturbing letters from her parents, who reported that more and more oppressive measures were being imposed on Koreans by the Japanese military. She urged, "Let us go and do what we can to help. We cannot let these measures continue unchecked!"

But the ladies shook their heads. They admired my mother for her unflagging patriotism and determination to take part in the plan. They said, "Hee Kyung, we think you should go and represent all of us. We will pay for your trip."

In the summer of 1918 my parents agreed that I, then three-and-a-half years old, should accompany my mother to Korea while my father stayed behind. Because I had been ill for months with the whooping cough, I was thin and frail.

"I'm concerned about Chung Sook," Father said. "Hee Kyung, don't you think you should wait until she's stronger?"

"But we may not reach Korea in time for the demonstration." She was torn. Finally she added, "My brother is a physician back home. You know, we can't afford a doctor here. But as soon as we get there I will put our daughter under his care."

The Youngnam Puin Hoe publicly announced to the immigrant community that Hee Kyung Kwon was their emissary to the demonstration, although the date for it was yet unknown. The Koreans responded with generous donations from their hard-earned wages to the cause, and the funds gathered were entrusted to my mother to take with her.

CHAPTER 2

For a Cause

OUR long trip from Honolulu to Korea began in the middle of July 1918. In the ship's steerage hold my mother proved to be a poor traveler by sea. She lay for days in her bunk unable to raise her head in the steamy, dark cabin, which was inhabited by scores of people. Both she and I were sick during most of the voyage.

The ship docked in a seaport in Japan; then we traveled by train and ferry and train again before we reached the city of Taegu.

My grandparents and many of our relatives were waiting for us at the train station. As soon as they met, my grandmother and my mother embraced each other and cried for a long time. Everyone wiped tears from their eyes, so happy were they to see us.

Grandmother sighed, "Let me look at you, Hee Kyung, and your daughter." Shaking her head, she called us *mal-lata* and *nu-reh,* so thin, scrawny, and pale. "Why?" she asked.

"I don't know. Hawaii is not like Taegu," Mother replied.

We all went to the home of my grandparents. Grandmother in her white *cho-gori* and *chi-ma* looked serene, and Grandfather appeared tall and dignified in a white robe and loose white pants. Older people traditionally wore white. Nobody but Mother seemed to mind the summer heat. Fanning herself, she noted, "I'd forgotten it gets so hot in Taegu." All the relatives crowded around my mother on the cool, matted floor, eager to hear about Hawaii.

After they left, two servant girls came into the sitting room with trays of food and set up a pair of small, black lacquer tables on the floor. My grandparents sat apart from us at their *sahng,* and my mother and I shared a *sahng.* We started with a refreshing cold soup, followed by small dishes of fish, vegetables, pickles, kim chee, and steaming rice. I felt as though I were at a feast and wondered whether we would eat so lavishly everyday.

For several days my grandparents listened intently to the purpose of my mother's trip. When visitors dropped in, they too listened and became seriously engrossed in her purpose.

Outside it was hotter than in the house. The family property was enclosed from the street and I could see people coming through a tall, wooden gate, either to visit us or to visit my uncle, Dr. Lee Han Bok, a physician, at his clinic. The clinic buildings stood on one side of the gate and the family living quarters on the other. Inside the gate lay a broad courtyard with a well in the center. The nurses and our servants drew water as they needed from this *u-mul.*

The rambling family quarters housed my grandparents and, next to them, my uncle and his wife and baby. Then the building turned at a right angle to the adjoining large kitchen and the servants' quarters beyond it. A narrow walkway protected by the roof started from the kitchen, passed my uncle's rooms, and stopped at my grandparents'.

I was taken to the clinic everyday, where my uncle examined me. He concluded after the first appointment that I was malnourished and in need of medication. He smiled and predicted that my cheeks would bloom and turn rosy in no time like the cheeks of all the other children in Korea.

After the first week of our arrival, my mother left the house each morning and was gone for most of the day. She was becoming reacquainted with friends she used to know, she told us, and she hinted at meeting some important people. Grandfather also went out everyday to a social hall where he spent the day with his friends. Like many of his companions, he was a descendant of a former government official. Officials, who were usually scholars turned politicians, were appointed by the

king and rewarded with considerable prestige and large land-
holdings. The ownership of the lands remained in the family
from generation to generation.

Grandfather dressed carefully like other city *yangban*—men
of leisure. He put on baggy white pants made of fine muslin,
gathered at the waist and at the ankle by drawstrings. Over the
pants he wore a flowing white tunic coat in shiny silk, which
overlapped in front like a robe and tied to the side with a bow. A
black, dome-shaped, narrow-brimmed hat made of silky horse-
hair was set on his head and secured with black ties under his
chin. On his feet he wore flat-soled rubber shoes shaped like
boats. In one hand he carried a long pipe for smoking, and in
his other hand a cane—the finishing touch to his dress. He
opened the gate and strutted off to a nearby meetinghouse.

Left at home, Grandmother and I often passed our time sit-
ting outside our rooms on the shaded edge of the veranda, fan-
ning ourselves. Sometimes the courtyard, which we viewed with
squinting eyes, blazed in the sun like a white sheet with a small,
dark speck at the center.

The evenings were not much cooler. I saw some people drag
their beds out to the street and sleep there, but Grandmother
would not let me even think of doing it.

One day I noticed an abrupt change in the usual routine.
Mother began preparing for a journey. "We're going to Andong
to visit your other grandparents," she said.

Then she wished to change her plans. The digression from
her normal routine was upsetting to her. Apparently she had
promised to visit more of her friends. She said to Grandmother,
"I think it's not a good time to make this trip. It's too hot. You
know, August is the hottest month of the year!"

Grandmother shook her head. "I think you should pay your
respects to your in-laws as soon as possible. Imagine how happy
they'll be to see their first grandchild."

"But, Omoni, both Chung Sook and I are so skinny. We
should wait. You said so yourself we look scrawny as beggars."

"No, you don't look that bad." Grandmother laughed and
dismissed the argument.

"Well, we can't visit too long. I must return soon for I have some unfinished business to attend to." Mother looked distracted. She did not seem pleased about meeting this obligation.

But I was excited. The next day I was dressed in a long, red silk *chi-ma* and multistriped *cho-gori*. I put on padded white cotton stockings and red embroidered shoes.

Mother dressed carefully. She wore a full, green, pleated *chi-ma,* which made a nice rustling sound when she walked. Her yellow silk *cho-gori* was tied in front with a graceful bow; the narrow embroidered trim in red around the neck and the tips of the sleeves matched the red embroidery on her canoe-shaped green shoes.

Six strong-looking men wearing loose, white muslin pants and shirts appeared outside our gate. They brought a palanquin —a sedan chair. The vehicle, a square box with a gently sloping roof that rose to a peak, was painted in festive colors of red and blue and yellow. There were gold tassels hanging from each corner of the roof.

Grandmother pointed at the palanquin. "Chung Sook, see that *kama?* You'll be riding it to Andong. It's your mother's idea to impress your other grandparents." I had once heard that a bride customarily rides in a *kama* to meet the groom and her in-laws on her wedding day.

On a cedar chest in our room was a picture of Ok Kyung, my mother's sister, in her wedding dress. She wore a beautiful ceremonial silk robe in bright red, gold, and green, with soft oversized striped sleeves extending over her wrists and hands. A small beaded ornament, which resembled a miniature crown, was perched on her head. A long bejeweled stick at the back of her neck held her braided black hair in place. Her skirt covered her shoes. Two round, red spots of color stood out on her masklike white face and her lips were painted red. I remembered that picture of my aunt, Ok Kyung, as a bride.

Mother and I entered the *kama* by pushing curtains apart through a side opening. The sedan chair rested on two long parallel poles. Four men lifted the straps of the chair onto their shoulders; the two relief men followed behind. The windows on all sides were covered with curtains, through which I could see the men in the front and the back. They were to cover the distance from Taegu to Andong in one day. Sometimes they ran together in fast, rhythmic steps and at other times in a slow horse trot.

The inside of the sedan chair was roomy enough for one passenger in a sitting position, but for the two of us it felt crowded. Korean silk trimmed the walls inside. Being careful of the gifts for my grandparents lying in one corner, I crawled around on the floor behind and beside my mother. She sat like a statue on the mat-covered floor, very still and quiet. She would not let me sit on her lap. "You will wrinkle my skirt!" she warned. At one time she scolded, "Chung Sook, you're crushing my dress!"

It grew hotter and hotter inside the *kama*. I could see the men had taken off their shirts and perspiration rolled like soft, fat beads down their bodies. Suddenly the *kama* began rocking, tilting to one side and then the other. I was rolling around until my mother's hand swung back to steady me. Whether I felt hunger or nausea I'm not sure. I screamed and cried. The *kama* stopped. One of the men poked his head in. He lifted me out and carried me in his arms. Although the sun shone directly overhead, I soon felt cooler and better and stopped crying.

Soon we crossed a shallow river and the men found a tree under which we could rest. From nowhere, it seemed, appeared *to shirak* lunches for the six men and my mother and me. We all sat under the tree and opened our boxes. The men ate noisily, pushing the rice and *banchan* into their mouths with wooden chopsticks.

It was almost dark when we finally reached our destination. My grandparents had been looking out for us all day, they said. At their door Mother bowed stiffly. I bowed, too. I was sorry my dress was so wrinkled.

Although my eyes were practically closed from the tiring journey, I noticed that my grandparents were stout and strong and their faces were sunbrown dark. They wore the traditional white clothes of old people.

The next day Mother told me that my father's parents were

nong jang juin, landowner farmers, who worked in the fields all day with their tenants. Their three big sons did not work alongside them because they spent almost all day attending school. When they came home late in the afternoon they took turns entertaining me.

One day my uncle, Sang Kyu, put me on his shoulders and started walking fast. He followed a trail leading to the hill behind the house.

"Where're we going, Ajusi?" I asked, holding on tight to his neck. He was the tallest of my uncles. I heard my mother say he was *jal-senggyut-suh.* Not only was he handsome but he had big, round eyes that seemed to be laughing all the time, although I did not hear him laugh very often.

"Chung Sookee," he said, "you'll see something wonderful today."

"Wonderful? What? Where?"

"You will soon see," he answered softly as we reached the end of the dirt trail and took the road to the park behind the hill.

Suddenly we came upon a lot of people in a festive mood. In the late afternoon the park lay partly shaded under the backdrop of rolling hills, while near the road the sun shone brightly. Children in gay holiday clothes were laughing and running after each other. There were groups of young men, like my uncles, running races while older men in white sat in groups under the trees, crooning and telling stories. Women's voices rose and fell in shrill excitement. Except for the older people, everybody was dressed in bright colors.

"What are those men over there doing?" I pointed to a group lined up facing bright, round boards set up against the rocks. Whenever they shouted, it was because someone had hit the target.

"Oh, those young men are engaged in the game called *hwal sogi.*"

Then we came upon some young women, laughing and squealing. They seemed to be having so much fun. Uncle stopped and said, "See those see-saw boards? And the ladies jumping on them?"

"Yes, yes!" I watched the young women with awe. They were leaping up and down on narrow boards, one at each end, gleefully soaring higher and higher into the air and, without missing, landing on the board in their shoes shaped like canoes.

The *nul-dwi-gi* board, about ten or eleven inches wide by seven feet long, was placed over a roll of grass matting. Two young women would climb onto the board, one at each end, and begin leaping up and down. Sometimes a third woman positioned herself at the center of the board to steady it.

Of course, the jumpers experienced numerous falls and accidents. But with great concentration they became highly skilled in the game. The *nul-dwi-gi* was a favorite pastime for young unmarried women, especially in the spring and fall. When flowers bloomed after a long winter, or just before the season of rain and snow, families went on picnics in the parks or in the countryside and set up the *nul-dwi-gi* board.

"Sookee, some day I hope you will do *nul-dwi-gi* like those ladies," Ajusi chuckled.

"Yes!" I cried. "I want to!"

The women reminded me of bright birds in the sky in their colorful *chi-ma* and *cho-gori,* their hair braided and tied with ribbons at the ends. I shivered with delight as I watched them.

My uncle told me, "This is *Chusuk,* a celebration of the farmers for their rich harvest. We begin a holiday season every year on August 15, by the lunar calendar. We honor our ancestors, visit each other's homes, eat, and rejoice in our good fortune. It is a happy time for several weeks."

When we walked past the old men I saw them sipping *sul* from tiny cups. Most of the older women were busy setting long tables with delicious food. I could smell the meats, fish, and chicken cooking on the stoves near the tables. The smoke from the wood stoves, thick and hazy, hung like billowy clouds over the tenders of the fire.

My mother and grandparents soon arrived with baskets filled with food to add to the already-laden tables. They placed mounds of *sangchu ssam,* kim chee *nu-reum jeok,* and many varieties of multicolored rice candies and pinenuts. On the tables were the Korean salads—*namul*—which were mild or peppery vegetables. My two other uncles came and joined us before the sun set.

After eating heartily, everybody started singing songs about working and harvesting in the fields.

After two weeks in Andong, Mother decided we should return to Taegu by train, which I found a faster and more comfortable way to travel.

As soon as we reached home, Mother hurried to resume "contacting her friends." Only at dinnertime did she pause to relate to her mother and father about the *Chusuk* holiday in Andong and tell them about her in-laws. I had more to tell. They enjoyed hearing about my uncles and how one of them carried me to a park where there were so many people. "I saw ladies jumping on the *nul-dwi-gi* and many small children." My grandparents laughed hard when I recounted my experience riding in the *kama*.

In September my mother decided to go to Seoul, the capital city. A week later she wrote to Grandmother that she was enrolling in Ewha College because that was where she found the people she needed to be with.

I did not know then that Ewha, a college for women, was seething with nationalism and that the majority of the students were revolutionaries. These young intellectual radicals detested the Japanese and were fomenting an overthrow of their rule. They secretly planned one day to join other political groups in the country in a massive show of patriotism.

"I don't know how long your mother will stay in Seoul," Grandmother said to me. "Shall we go and visit her?"

"Yes, yes," I answered. This was the first time I had been separated from my mother and I missed her.

One day in October when the weather was clear, with no anticipation of rain or snow, Grandmother and I, accompanied by one of the servant girls, Sook Cha, took the train to Seoul.

When we met my mother in her dormitory room, we found her in a blue military uniform. How strange she looked without her *chi-ma* and *cho-gori*. She removed the blue cap from her head and sat on the floor, crossing her legs as a man would. I wanted to be close to her and climbed on her lap.

"I'm so sorry you can't be with me every day, Chung Sook," she sighed, stroking my head.

"Please come home, Omoni," I begged.

Her chin grew hard. She looked tense. "Chung Sook, I can't. We're almost ready." She did not explain.

Grandmother seemed to understand. She did not say much. She did not try to persuade Mother to return home. She merely stared at her daughter with sad eyes.

Back in Taegu we waited anxiously for word from Mother. There were few letters. During the day Grandmother read books to me or chatted with me. I was learning to speak Korean fluently. Either she or Sook Cha took me to the clinic for my checkups with my uncle.

One day I thought I would visit my uncle by myself. Wandering through a maze of rooms in the clinic, I saw a door ajar. I walked into the room. A woman lay on a stack of large pillows with a sheet thrown over her knees. When she happened to see me, she snapped, "What are you doing here, child!" I froze for a second. Then, without answering, I turned and ran. I hurriedly retraced my steps and ran out of the clinic.

Fewer and fewer letters were coming from Seoul. My grandparents often spoke quietly together as if they were sharing a deep secret. I was disappointed when my fourth birthday came in November and my mother was not home to celebrate with us.

Several months passed. One day I was aware of a tense, cloying stillness hanging in the air. I was confused. I felt as if everyone were waiting for something dreadful to happen. Grandmother seemed preoccupied and did not care to entertain me. For long periods she merely sat on a flat pillow on the floor with needlework in her hands, which she barely looked at. Her usually serene face wore a frown—two little lines between her eyes.

"Why won't you talk to me, Grandma?" I asked several times. She'd turn to me and look as if she was about to say something, then stare off into space and forget to answer. I amused myself the best I could; because the weather was bad I could not go outside.

When the servant girl set up the low *sahng* and served our evening meal, Grandmother hardly touched her food. Nor did she prod me to eat as was her habit. Grandfather sat stolid at his own *sahng* and dined without his usual chatter. For some reason, he had not gone out that day.

I wondered what my grandparents were waiting for. They reminded me of frightened children who expected something terrible to happen to them because they had been naughty.

Suddenly we were jolted by a knock on the door.

"Nu gu si o?" Grandfather demanded. "Who are you?"

"Bong Chu it is, sir," came the reply. I recognized the voice of one of our servants.

Grandmother quickly rose and pushed open the papered sliding door. Gusts of icy wind blew into the room while Bong Chu removed his shoes. He walked in wearing his thick, padded white stockings. There was some snow still clinging to his coat and hair. His eyes were very wide, like those of a scared animal. Had he been naughty, I wondered?

He bowed respectfully. Then the words rushed out of his mouth: "Today, March 1, 1919, is a bad day for Korea! The Japanese have killed so many of our people!" Bong Chu began to sob.

"Ai gu, ai gu!" my grandparents moaned in shock.

"A-ni-o!" Grandmother cried. "No, no! Not my daughter, Hee Kyung!" She held her fists together tight as if in anguished prayer.

"A-ni-o," Bong Chu said, comforting her. "I saw your daughter. She was marching near the front of the parade. Hundreds and hundreds—maybe thousands—of people lined the streets to watch. They shouted, *'Man sei! Man sei!'* Then the Japanese police came. They beat up the crowd—everybody in their path. They cut down our Korean flags the marchers carried. They

used sabers, sticks, and rifles! It was terrible! People were falling all around. Blood on the street. Everybody trying to scatter and escape. And your daughter—I saw her. She was shoved into a police wagon with many others. I think she's in jail now."

"*Ai gu, ai gu. U chak ko?*" Both my grandparents looked helpless. "What shall we do?"

I was not able to follow Bong Chu's account. I asked, "What's happened to my mother? Is she coming home soon?"

Grandmother turned to me and beckoned. Tears were streaming down her cheeks. I moved over and sat next to her.

She spoke quietly, "Bong Chu, thank you for the news. You had a long journey to Seoul today. Were there many people on the trains?"

"Yes, so many! I had to push my way to get on one. Every train was packed." Bong Chu's flat young face was flushed. He was moving his body as if he were still on the train.

"Go now and have your supper." Grandmother motioned him to leave. Bong Chu bowed and went out the door.

The tense stillness of March 1 lingered through the next few days. Grandfather stayed at home. No one dared to go out to the street. The military commander's curfew rule forced people to remain in their homes.

But our servants were able to tread the back alleys and gather information, and they reported what they heard to my grandparents. They learned that the demonstrations for independence had taken place all over Korea, even in the small towns and outlying provinces. The largest parade, it was believed, was in Seoul. Thousands had joined in the marches, waved flags, cried for justice and an end to Japanese oppression. When the police started shooting and slaughtering the marchers, the Koreans wildly destroyed or damaged custom houses, police stations, and court buildings, especially those in the outskirts of the capital. The Japanese angrily retaliated by setting fire to many Korean churches and schoolhouses.

How quickly and brutally the Japanese suppressed the revolutionists! During the parade in Seoul a young woman's hand, proudly waving the Korean flag, was cut off by a Japanese sword. But before the flag touched the ground, she caught it with her other hand. More than 2,500 Koreans were thrown in prison in Seoul alone that day. Among the women activists incarcerated was my mother, Lee Hee Kyung.

The night after Bong Chu's return from Seoul I asked Grandmother, "When will my omoni come home?" She did not answer me.

I put my hands on the sides of her face and begged, "Halmuni, look at me. Please tell me."

She took my small hands in hers. "Chung Sook, your mother . . . is . . . in prison now. I don't know when . . ."

"In prison? Can we go to visit her? Remember, we went to the dormitory to see her."

Grandmother's eyes grew watery. "No, I'm sorry, we can't. I don't know when . . . it's too dangerous now. We must wait."

"Wait until tomorrow?"

She broke into a laugh. Her lips spread in a smile. She extended a finger and said, "You are a child. You don't understand." Then her smile swiftly passed. She sat upright and ran a hand over her dress, as if she had to be ready to meet some one or some event.

I was disappointed. Both my grandparents were continually preoccupied. Grandpa sat in a corner and brooded with his mouth thrust forward, as if he had words to say but he wouldn't let them out. Because it was snowing, I could not go out to play.

Then the servants reported that they heard the police had caught and imprisoned Choe Namson, who was known to have almost singlehandedly drafted the Korean Declaration of Independence. Also, all thirty-three leaders who had signed the declaration had voluntarily surrendered to Japanese authorities soon after the mass demonstration.

One man who was involved with the independence movement was Tough Chin Ho. I met him about fifty years later in Honolulu when he was ninety years old. He declared that the demonstration on March 1 had turned out badly, not at all as he had expected. "We originally planned to stage our demonstration on the third of March—the third day of the third month. But there was a sudden change of plans and I was not able to attend for I was at my school in the country."

Mr. Tough sighed, "We really thought our uprising would catch the attention and sympathy of the United States, Britain, Holland, and the other big powers of the world. Once they learned of our plight we were sure they would come to our rescue. But no such help came. The nations declared it was an internal matter for the Japanese and they would not interfere. Koreans suffered worse conditions after our failed attempt to gain liberty. The Japanese became more cruel and oppressive. They banned political meetings, gatherings of any kind."

He continued, "I had been working closely with Pak Sung Woo and Kim Young Phum, who escaped to Shanghai where the Korean Provisional government was established. I had to join Pak and Kim, but I had to be careful. I was the principal of a school. I knew the Japanese military suspected I was an activist. They were watching my every move. I made an attempt to get out of the country one night."

"I packed a bag, took my horse, and headed for Soon Chun to bid goodbye to my mother. A policeman accosted me. 'Why are you leaving your school?' he asked. I said, 'I'm going to visit my mother. She is not well. I plan to spend a few days with her.' Not believing me, he ordered, 'Follow me to the station.'

"It was a dark night. When we came to a river, the officer and his horse got in front of me on the bridge. I followed. I knew I would be thrown in jail if the military found a copy of the independence document on me. The officer did not see me pull the document out of my pocket and drop it into the river. We reached the station and the staff searched me and my bag. I insisted I was innocent, had nothing to do with Korea's fight for independence. They released me that night.

"Shortly after that incident, I managed to get out of Korea and join Pak and Kim."

Tough added wistfully, "I wish I had been present in Seoul on March 1. You can imagine the high excitement that day. At two o'clock in the afternoon the demonstrators assembled in Pagoda Park in the heart of the city. Copies of the independence declaration signed by thirty-three men were passed out by students. Copies were simultaneously being distributed in the neighboring towns and provinces by students who had gone there from Seoul. The declaration was read to the cheering crowd in the park. Thousands of Korean flags appeared, shouts of *Man sei! Man sei!* went up, and then the people burst out into the streets in a huge parade. No one carried arms. It was intended to be a peaceful demonstration to show we Koreans have the mind and the spirit of a free nation.

"At first the Japanese military was stunned. Then they became alarmed. They could not believe their subjects dared to revolt, much less wave Korean flags. To save their pride, the Japanese massacred thousands of our countrymen, wounded and arrested thousands more.

"One thing was accomplished on that terrible day: Koreans were galvanized as a unified people who would dream of liberty and pursue that dream until independence was finally won."

My grandparents continued to worry about my mother. "What can she be eating in prison?" Grandma mumbled to herself. "I know Hee Kyung never liked Japanese food."

"I hope they're at least feeding the prisoners," Grandpa grunted. "I've never seen the inside of the Seoul jailhouse. I've heard from some men who were incarcerated for some silly offense that it's dark and filthy. Can you imagine Hee Kyung in such a place?"

Grandmother added, "And it must be so crowded in there. How many did they say were captured? I believe all of those that weren't slain."

Day after day, month after month, we waited and prayed and hoped for Mother's eventual release from prison.

CHAPTER 3

Two Prison Terms

MARCH, April and then May passed before those who were incarcerated in the March 1 uprising were gradually let out of prison. What happy news! We waited with high anticipation for my mother's return home. My grandmother heard from many of her excited relatives and friends in Seoul, Pusan, and Taegu, that their husbands and their children who had been jailed were released. In the following months—June, July, August—many more prisoners were freed. The Japanese boasted of having let thousands go. But my mother was not one of the fortunate ones.

The winter of 1919 was bleak and sad at our house. My grandparents could not understand why the military was holding the rest of the revolutionaries. "The police have declared the streets of Korea are safe now that there are no more insurgents and rioters," Grandfather said. Then he added, "I wonder if they know that Hee Kyung is from Hawaii and suspect that she represents a powerful organization."

Grandmother argued softly, "But she told us the Youngnam Puin Hoe is made up of only a small group of women, all poor immigrants."

"The Japanese are just suspicious people; *Mang-hal-num!*" he cursed the enemy. "Can they be detaining her because they're afraid she'll start another revolt?" Grandfather's anger was rising and his face turned a deep red.

Grandmother no longer looked serene these days; she continually wore a frown—little lines between her eyes. Addressing my grandfather with the familiar word for spouse, she said, "Yobo, I'm afraid the police must have found the list of donors to the cause which, you remember, our daughter always carried with her on her money belt." Grandmother was suddenly overcome with dismay and anguish, and she covered her face.

Most Korean men and women carried their money and other valuables next to their bodies under their clothing. They hung the purse from a belt, and the belt was tied to the body before they put on the dress for the day.

Grandfather hissed, "*Mang-hal-num!* Of course they would think nothing of shaming our daughter by ordering her to disrobe." He stood up and, shaking his head, walked around the room, muttering, "Why does Hee Kyung involve herself in political matters? Why can't she be like her sister, just . . . just a quiet lady at home . . ."

With the lifting of the curfew by the military commander after the March 1 revolution, my grandfather resumed his habit of leaving the house early each morning to spend the day with his friends. For weeks, when the weather permitted, I waited outside at the gate for my mother's return so I could be the first to greet her.

I enjoyed watching the stream of people passing by our gate; we lived on one of the busy streets of Taegu. I saw big, stately women carrying tall water jugs on their heads, measuring their steps as if keeping time to a march. There were younger women who moved nimbly, balancing on their heads straw baskets full of produce from the market. There were also servant girls bearing bundles of laundry, going to some mountain stream or river to do their washing; they did not have far to go, for Korea is a country with many streams and rivers.

Occasionally horse-drawn wagons driven by men wielding whips rolled by. The men's sing-song patter filled the air as they called out their wares: pots and pans, silks and cottons, needles and threads; also toys for children and medicine for the elderly. The slow clip-clop of the horses' hoofs accompanied the men's songs.

The wagon with offensive collections from the outhouses could be smelled by everyone before it was spotted down the road. The pedestrians drew as far away from it as possible when it passed by. The refuse was delivered miles away to country farmers for use as fertilizer.

One morning as I was munching on an apple I saw six or seven beggars lying asleep or crawling on the edge of the road. They were dirty and grimy. Their clothing was in tatters. I wondered how they were able to keep warm during the wintry nights. They swung their heads back and forth in a strange manner, their eyes darting this way and that. Were they looking for food? I felt like scolding these men and telling them to go home and wash up. Suddenly one of them turned and leaped toward me. Panic-stricken, I slammed the gate shut and ran to my grandmother. When I related to her what had happened, she advised, "You must be careful, Chung Sook. That beggar probably was going to snatch the apple from your hand. We don't have as many beggars here in Taegu as in Seoul. Still you must be careful."

The days grew shorter and colder. Soon it was November and my fifth birthday came and went. My mother again missed my birthday, the second since I arrived in Korea. A terrible gloom descended over our house and settled in our hearts. Grandmother began moaning a refrain over and over again about the loss of her daughter; occasionally she cried *"Ai gu! Ai gu!"* then started the woeful refrain again.

Life went on. In the morning a servant girl brought a jug of water for my grandparents and me to wash our faces. The girl then folded our cotton bedding and stacked it on low rosewood tables and cedar chests. The beautiful blankets, which were covered in silks of deep blues and reds, bright yellows, and shiny greens, shimmered and brightened our rooms all day.

My grandmother and I sat together and shared a low lacquer table for our meals while my grandfather had his own table. Our breakfast consisted of soup, rice, and kim chee. Another kind of soup came with our lunch and still another for dinner.

Several small dishes of *banchan* usually accompanied our meals. We did not eat meat very often. However, three or four different varieties of delicious kim chee always appeared with the *banchan*.

No meal in Korea was complete without kim chee. These spicy, colorful dishes with pieces of red chili pepper floating in the sauce made all the other dishes at the table taste wonderful. I learned to enjoy the very sharp, hot flavor—the hotter the tastier, I thought. I didn't mind if I bit into a garlic bud or slices of ginger or torn pieces of red pepper. I didn't mind the burning sensation on my tongue or in my throat.

Because of the lack of refrigeration, kim chee was made every few days. Fresh vegetables, such as cabbage, turnip, cucumber, and other greens, were salted, rinsed, then combined with kim chee sauce. Some people liked the sour, fermented kim chee but it was scorned by many who did not care for the "overripe."

Each year Koreans looked forward to eating "winter kim chee." Large quantities of this special kim chee were made in the fall, then packed in oversized crocks and buried under the snow. On our property a special kim chee hut was built, which was shaped like an inverted cone. It had no doors. The snow blew into the hut and kept the crocks, which were stacked deep in layers, covered with snow. This aged, frozen, fermented kim chee gave off a most pungent odor when it was brought to room temperature. From November to April we enjoyed this kim chee. Its taste was biting and its memory unforgettable.

Sometimes Grandmother read stories to me. But during the long days of my mother's confinement in prison she was inclined to read to herself—leaning against an old cedar chest, forgetting about me. One day I noticed she hardly turned the pages of the book in her hand.

I was bored. I asked, "Halmuni, may I go to the *bu uk?*" She nodded. I was sure to find a lot of excitement in the kitchen.

As I neared the *bu uk* I heard the clatter of cooking utensils and very loud voices. Two of the girls were clashing over something. I paused for a moment. I could tell Sook Cha and Pil

Soon were quarreling, but I told myself I had no reason to be upset. Our servants always sounded as if they were involved in a disagreement or a terrible crisis or a huge joke. Usually hearty laughter followed and punctuated whatever they said to each other. It seemed they laughed over everything and nothing.

When I entered the kitchen a chorus of welcome greeted me: "Chung Sook, Chung Sook, come, come!" Two women, standing over huge pots of soup on the open woodstove, were singing a duet. Several young girls were on the floor peeling garlic buds or slicing vegetables or removing bones from dried fish. Three men lounged lazily against the wall; during the winter their activities were limited to running errands, delivering messages or bringing in the firewood. But during the spring, summer, and fall they worked long hours on the family farm beyond the courtyard, planting and harvesting fruits and vegetables. They brought the produce to the kitchen and took to market what was not needed at home.

Watching the woman pounding the laundry fascinated me. She sat at the foot of the steps. Each time she beat down with her smooth stick on the clothes soaking in the round tub, soap water splattered all around her. There was laundry to do every day, with boiling water for the whites and cold water for the rinse.

I often played with the children of the servants. When the weather permitted, we played in the courtyard. During the winter, throwing snowballs at each other was our favorite pastime.

Finally, word reached my grandparents of the discharge of most if not all Koreans captured on the day of the ill-fated demonstration. After nearly a year in prison my mother was coming home!

On a cold January morning in 1920 a small woman with her head bowed came slowly through the gate. Our servant Bong Chu was there to let her in.

"Omoni! Omoni!" I cried, and ran to meet her. She held me and wept. Over and over she murmured, "Sookee, Sookee," I was crying too, although I was so happy.

Grandmother rushed out of the house. She tried to speak but her greeting was lost in tears. She could only hold my mother in her arms. Grandfather, who joined us out at the gate, shed no tears. Instead he shouted one curse after another at the Japanese: *"Weh-num, weh-num! Mang-hal-num! Do dong num!"*

As we went into the sitting room, I noticed my grandmother did not look particularly happy. "Halmuni, aren't you glad my mother has come home? Why do you look so sad?"

"Because your mother is so thin and frail. She is nothing but skin and bone!"

Smiling weakly, Mother said, "Omoni, don't worry about me. I'm back. I will be fine soon."

"Yes," Grandmother agreed quickly, "Of course you will be fine. You will rest and eat and do nothing else."

"No, there's something I must do." Straightening herself, Mother surprised everyone when she said, "Chung Sook and I must prepare to leave as soon as possible for Hawaii. Her father must be very lonely."

Grandmother could not believe what she heard. She said, "We'll talk about this later," and dismissed the subject.

We were interrupted by the servants who wished to pay their respects to the master's daughter. The young women appeared very well-dressed that morning, looking more like guests at a party. Their gay, cheerful greetings and quick smiles made my mother forget momentarily the suffering and weariness of her past year. She thought the girls looked like identical dolls, with their black hair parted in the middle and combed smoothly back, their duplicate pleated green *chi-ma* and yellow *cho-gori* freshly pressed. They asked Mother if they could bring her some soup and fruits. Mother's eyes opened wide with pleasure when she saw the plump, luscious pears and persimmons and the crisp apples. She enjoyed the *meeyuk kuk,* a nourishing seaweed soup.

The Japanese Imperial Government stringently controlled all those entering and leaving the country because Koreans were subjects of the emperor. Although she had lived in Hawaii, which was a territory of the United States, my mother was not an American citizen. She wanted to obtain a passport as quickly as possible, but she encountered unexpected delay at the Immigration Office. The officials there not only refused to issue the passport but gave no assurance that it would ever be given to her.

When my grandfather heard of this, his cynicism grew; with his contempt for the Japanese increasing, he predicted that the military commander would detain his daughter indefinitely.

One day he returned from the meetinghouse and reported what he called "the lastest damnable rule of the Japanese." Since he and his friends could read the Japanese newspapers they were apprised of the enemy's latest plots to harass the Koreans.

"Now we must speak Japanese all the time. Our children will study the language and use it in school. In the marketplace and on the street we must not be caught speaking in Korean."

A few days later he told us, "Japan is keeping track of the Korean National Independence Movement, which is starting all over the world, especially in Hawaii, and on the West Coast of the United States, and in Shanghai and Manchuria." But he became sober when he thought of its effect on my mother's situation. "I can see the military really has reason now to detain Hee Kyung. They wouldn't want her to go back to Hawaii and add fuel to the movement."

For Mother and me the wait for permission to leave Korea was incredibly long. We spent one whole year and part of the next hoping and praying for a change in the commander's orders. Finally, in July 1921, we received the official word that we could leave for Hawaii!

Then began the hurried but joyous preparations for the long journey home. Grandmother purchased silks and cottons of the finest quality for dresses and blankets. The servants packed all kinds of delicious foods, including kim chee. For her friends Mother bought pretty shoes, some with embroidery on silk. She received gifts of silver spoons and chopsticks, brass bowls for soup and rice, and carved figurines of the *yangban* and old women, and scenic scrolls and family pictures to take home with us.

Every day our home was filled with well-wishers. Young women, who adored my mother, laughed and cried together, and recounted their struggles and suffering during their activist days. They declared that their friend radiated joy and happiness. "Hee Kyung, you are laughing again. Your eyes are so small they look closed when you laugh!"

Just two days before our scheduled departure in August, four of Mother's dearest friends surprised us by offering to accompany us as far as Yokohama, where we would catch a steamer bound for Honolulu. We were touched. Together we traveled to Japan.

None of us expected the turn of events that started at the Yokohama Immigration Office. The officials there claimed they recognized the name of my mother as a rioter and a disturber of peace in Seoul. In fact, the names of the four friends with us were also on their records as rebels and participants in a riot. A trial was held. They were all found guilty of rioting and ordered to serve a prison term in Yokohama.

Only the youngest of them, nineteen-year-old Hee Soon, was allowed to remain free so that she could chaperon me while my mother and the three other women were imprisoned. Hee Soon had walked in the ill-fated parade but she was excused because she had been only a high school student then.

I called Hee Soon *ajumani,* which means aunt. Day after day she and I waited in a dingy hotel in Yokohama. Because she could read and speak Japanese we had no trouble finding our way around in the city or ordering food in a restaurant. We took a rickshaw one day and went to the Yokohama Harbor to view the ships, on one of which my mother and I might sail to Honolulu.

We made a disturbing visit to the jail one day to see my mother. When we arrived there, Ajumani and I were asked to wait because the Korean women had to "finish their chores" before they could see us.

"Look over there!" Ajumani suddenly cried, pointing to the far end of a vast, vacant hall near which we were sitting.

I couldn't believe what I saw. Four women in rumpled *chi-ma* and *cho-gori* were on their hands and knees, pushing large, wet wads of rags up and down the long, vacant hall. With loose strands of hair falling over their faces, their long skirts tangling under their legs, they looked like hard-working servants! Near them drowsed two guards, lazily tilting their chairs back against the wall. When the moppers noticed me and Ajumani they burst out laughing.

Later, on the way back to the hotel, I asked Ajumani, "Wasn't that hard work? But Omoni and the other ladies were laughing. Do you think they were having fun?"

"No! Of course not," Ajumani answered with vehemence. "Your mother and her friends were so embarrassed and ashamed, they didn't know what else to do." She added under her breath, "Those stupid, demeaning *weh-num*. How I loathe them!"

Weeks passed. Ajumani and I continued to wait. Sometimes we went window-shopping, but nothing in the shops interested us. The hotel bills were mounting.

One day Ajumani looked extremely sad. She kept staring out the window and avoiding me. She wasn't really watching the busy pedestrian traffic below nor the wagons and rickshaws. The sky was filled with dark clouds. We rarely saw the sun in Yokohama.

After a while I asked, "What's the matter, Ajumani?"

Slowly she turned to face me. She began, "Chung Sook, I don't like to say this."

"Say what?"

She bit her lip. Then she said softly, "I think I'll have to take you back to Taegu to your Grandmother's."

"What! Why?"

"I'm so sorry. We don't know how long the Japanese will hold your mother and our friends in prison. It might be a long, long time. Perhaps . . . it would be better for you to go and stay with your grandparents."

"No! I don't want to. I want to stay here near my mother. I want to go back to Hawaii with her to see my father."

"Yes, I know, Chung Sook." She sighed, her voice trailed, "We'll see . . ."

There were more weeks of waiting after that.

Then one day without any advance notice, by some fluke, the immigration officials arbitrarily freed the Korean women. My mother and her three friends looked tired and angry, but they managed to smile when they passed by the officers in the prison. They had been incarcerated for almost two months.

Quickly all the gifts and foods we had brought with us were gathered together. Kim chee and fish odors permeated our rooms, although Ajumani and I had not been aware of the pickled and marinated foods while they were hidden from view in the closet.

On the next available steamer bound for Honolulu I went aboard with my mother. As we climbed up the gangplank we waved a tearful goodbye to our four dear, sad friends standing on the Yokohama pier, waving white handkerchiefs.

CHAPTER 4

The Tragic Split

RETURNING to Hawaii, we were again passengers in the dark steerage hold of a ship. My mother was confined to her bunk for most of the fortnight journey; she said she could not bear the smells of so many people herded together in the three-tiered bunks, sweating, vomiting, and eliminating. Day after day I watched patiently over her. I wished I could go out of the crowded cabin for some fresh air but I dared not leave her.

One day she sat up and remarked, "Your father will be surprised to see how tall you've grown, Chung Sook. You and I have been away over three years."

I tried to visualize my father. I couldn't. Only the faces of my grandparents, my aunts and uncles, the servants, and our friends in Korea could I recall.

"Will Abuji be at the pier when we arrive in Honolulu?" I asked.

"Of course your father will be there. He'll be so happy to see us!"

At last our ship entered Honolulu Harbor. "There's your father!" Mother cried, lifting me to the railing of the ship as it docked. She pointed to a man standing at the edge of a cluster of people. His hair was cut very short and he wore a dark suit. He waved; a quiver of nervous anticipation ran through me. I put up my hand to wave back but held it in mid-air, for the man standing below was a stranger.

We went down to the foot of the gangplank and waited for him. As he strode toward us he looked bigger than I had thought from my place at the ship's railing.

His face abruptly broke into a smile and his eyes lighted up with gladness. He shook hands with Mother and patted me on the back.

The Korean men and women who had come on the ship with us greeted their spouses and friends with handshakes while the Japanese people bowed low and did not touch each other. All the men on the pier wore grey or black suits, except for a few Japanese men in dark kimonos. All the women were in their native dress—bright *chi-ma* and *cho-gori* or multihued kimonos.

Father announced proudly to Mother, "Yobo, I've rented a house on Iolani Avenue. I think you will like it."

She looked pleased and asked, "How many rooms does it have?"

"Two bedrooms. A parlor, kitchen, and bathroom."

Our house was the second from the top of four identical-looking cottages built in a row on a sloping street. They were separated from each other by about five feet all around.

We had to walk with care around the colorfully wrapped gifts and many jars of food from Korea, which filled the small living room. In each bedroom was a brown chest and a high, white iron bed. When I sat on my bed it squeaked.

When I walked into the bathroom, the white toilet intrigued me, as did the wash basin that had a pipe with running water. I soon realized we did not need a maid to bring us water to wash our faces or to empty our chamber pots.

Mother stood in the kitchen a long time without saying a word. She looked lost and a little distressed. Finally, shaking her head, she muttered, "*Ai gu,* I'll have to start cooking again."

Father showed her where he kept the pots and pans, and together they prepared supper. He washed the rice and set the pot on the stove, and Mother selected an assortment of *banchan* from the jars and boxes on the living room floor. We sat on wooden stools around a small, unpainted table in the kitchen and enjoyed *kan-jang* fish, strips of peppery dried fish, pickled cucumbers, and pungent "overripe" kim chee.

As I was about to fall asleep the first night I overheard my father say, his voice tinged with sadness, "I wonder if our country will ever become a free nation."

Mother replied with passion, "Oh, we can't give up. We must find a way to defeat Japan."

In the next few days a stream of visitors, most of whom were members of the Korean Methodist Church, dropped in to see us. They talked about the Sam-il Woon Dong, the new term coined for the famous demonstration of March 1, 1919.

"You were so brave, Mrs. Kwon," they exclaimed and heaped praises on my mother for her years of suffering and her loyalty to the cause.

While the callers knew of her past revolutionary efforts, they did not seem to share her present feelings. She was puzzled. She heard that the once-powerful Korean National Association (KNA), which was the headquarters for all independence activities, had lost its influence. Its paid membership of 2,300 at the height of the independence fervor had plummeted to about 150 supporters by 1921, the year of our return.

When she returned to Hawaii, my mother was ready to rebuild and spread the flame of patriotism the Japanese had tried to smother by imprisoning her. To her surprise and dismay she realized that not only her husband but all the Methodists had lost their passion for their country's liberation. They looked beaten and lost.

How happy Mother was to see her dear friends, the members of the Youngnam Puin Hoe. She and I were honored guests at their first meeting after our return. The ladies were delighted with my accounts of life in Taegu and the people there.

They clapped their hands and cried, "Hee Kyung, your daughter speaks our language so beautifully!" Mother beamed.

The president, a stout woman wearing thick, dark-rimmed glasses, called the meeting to order. "Let us hear from the bravest in our society. Let us hear about her dramatic role in the Sam-il Woon Dong and the days, weeks, and months she spent in prison—our own Lee Hee Kyung." The society members were proud to use their maiden names when they were together, as it was the custom in Korea for married women.

My mother gave a long and vivid account of her sojourn of

the last three years. The ladies responded intermittently with *"Ai gu! Ai gu!"* or *"Kuh reh?"* in a questioning tone or *"Kuh reh!"* in affirmation. Several times they shouted, *"Mang-hal-num, mang-hal-num!"* Some of them, overcome with emotion, wiped away tears and blew their noses. At the end of her talk she exhorted them to waken to the cry of liberty. "Let us renew our efforts!"

The members squirmed in their chairs and looked confused. For once these women, who usually chatted and laughed incessantly when they were together, seemed to have nothing to say or laugh about.

My mother was perplexed. She asked, "Have you lost your zeal? Why are you so quiet?"

Then one woman started to explain. Pain lined her sensitive, pensive face. "We don't know how it all happened, Hee Kyung. While you were gone, Koreans here have been fighting. We've lost our leader—you remember that man we all loved so much, Yongman Park. He was banished by the governor and we think he has departed to Shanghai. And out Methodist church is split; half of our members have left for the church where Syngman Rhee preaches. And all the money we poured into the KNA for Korea's liberation—we don't know where it all went. There's been so much talk! And so much fighting!"

A woman interrupted, "Yes, and do you know there's even been fistfights in front of the Korean National Association building!" She gestured, flailing her arms: "The police were called. We heard that the *Advertiser* reported the news in the paper and the Americans heard about the fights. I was so ashamed."

A small, thin woman added in a conciliatory voice, "I know you must be terribly disappointed with us. This community is split in politics and in religion. We can't seem to agree on how to gain our independence or who to follow as leader."

"Yes, it's sad," agreed another lady. "Hee Kyung, you must feel that all you did was in vain. We're sorry. I wish we could think of a way to unify the factions and bring the two churches together."

"That'll never happen!" several ladies declared flatly.

All of a sudden the room turned into a hubbub of noise as everybody began talking at once, arguing, explaining, giving advice.

What my mother heard that day at the Youngnam Puin Hoe was the heartbreaking story of the collision of two volatile Korean scholars who came to Hawaii to lead the Korean immigrants. They knew the immigrants loved their country so much they would be willing to die to regain it. But the philosophies of these two men were incompatible and their personalities clashed. Each man attracted hundreds of loyal supporters. By some odd, accidental strokes of luck or fate, one succeeded and the other was disgraced.

The Korean National Association, needing a bright young man to head the association, had invited Yongman Park, a graduate of the University of Nebraska with a degree in political science. He with a group of his friends had established the Korean Youth Army School at Kearney Farm, Nebraska. He arrived in Honolulu in 1912. The KNA was pleased with Park's work as head of the organization and as editor of the *United Korean News*.

Initially the KNA was involved in diplomatic activities for Korea and in the education of its members' children. But after the annexation of Korea in 1910, the KNA turned more of its attention to collecting funds to relieve the plight of their countrymen under Japanese domination.

Park was articulate and appealing. He attracted the women especially, who thought he looked dashing in a military uniform. Many women named their newborn sons after him. His lifelong ambition was to lead a military army into Korea and rout the Japanese.

In 1913 Syngman Rhee, who was a delegate from Korea to a Methodist conference in Minnesota, contacted Park and begged him for a position in the KNA so that he could remain in the United States. Park obliged. Upon his arrival, Rhee immediately resented working under the aegis of his friend. Rhee connived ways to showcase his own leadership qualities; he was criticized and despised by some people for the cunning, skillful methods he used to achieve his ambition—to be the Korean leader with the largest following. Only seven months after his initial connection with the KNA, Rhee started publishing a monthly called the *Pacific Magazine* in which he criticized the management of the KNA and personally attacked Park. Hundreds of KNA members rose in protest against Park and joined Rhee's attack. Less than two years after he was invited by Park, Rhee succeeded in usurping his friend's position as head of the KNA.

In the meantime Park had started to build an army of sugarcane laborers in Kahaluu, on the island of Oahu. The small band of volunteers rose early each morning and reported for training. Patriotism ran high and the men were fiercely loyal to Park. The trainees willingly paid for their uniforms and equipment.

This military activity was to be kept a secret. But word soon leaked out to the Japanese Consul in Hawaii. Alarmed, Consul Matsuoka called on the governor of the Territory of Hawaii, Lucius E. Pinkham, and pointed to the danger of the Koreans being trained to bear arms. Obviously, the consul gave no hint of his own fear that a Korean army could pose a threat to Japan's rule in Korea.

Heeding the consul's warning, Governor Pinkham ordered Park to halt all military exercises. By 1916 Park's dream of a military force to take to Korea came to an end in Hawaii. He was banished to Shanghai. However, few people were aware of the governor's action until years later; while Park was the head of the KNA, he had been traveling back and forth to Shanghai, where the Korean Provisional Government in exile was established.

After he was ousted from the KNA, Yongman Park started his own political group and called it Dong Nip Dan (Korean Independence League). The league's purposes were to collect donations for the motherland's independence and to support those persons working for the cause. The league was organized on March 3, 1919; within a week the enrollment reached 350, and most of them, like Park, were Methodists. Then Park began publishing a weekly called the *Pacific Times,* to counteract Rhee's monthly publication, the *Pacific Magazine.* Syngman Rhee took up Park's challenge and formed his own political party, the Dong Ji Hoe (Comrade Society). The bulk of its membership was made up of members from his church, the Korean Christian Church.

His most cherished dream, Rhee said, was to educate the children of the immigrants. In fact, education was revered by all Koreans, and scholars had always been held in the highest esteem in their country.

The Methodist Board of Missions in Hawaii, which operated the Korean Compound School for Boys on Punchbowl Street, asked Rhee to serve as its principal. The Methodist Board was pleased to know that Rhee had received a doctorate from Princeton University. It was shortly after he had arrived in Hawaii in 1913 to join the KNA that he started serving at the school.

Rhee extended an invitation to Korean girls to attend the school, yet to his surprise the board strenuously objected and refused them admission. The girls, who were coming from plantation families outside of the city of Honolulu and from the outer islands, needed a place to stay. Rhee hastily decided to start a small school for them in Puunui and called the institution the Korean Girls' Seminary.

In need of money to support the new school Rhee went into the community for donations. The board reproved him for soliciting funds for a cause outside of the church domain and without its sanction. All along Rhee had been offering his services as principal at the Compound School without remuneration, as did most of the school staff who had arrived from the U.S. mainland to serve as missionaries.

He could not tolerate the board's protests and its refusal to educate girls of Korean ancestry. Later in the year 1916, Rhee, angry and weary of the board's opposition to his beliefs and actions, resigned as principal of the Compound School.

He thought he should abandon everything that had to do with Methodists. Religion was important to him and his countrymen, but he wanted to belong to a church in no way affiliated with the strong Methodist Board of Missions in Hawaii. So he started a new church in 1916, called it the Korean Christian Church, and began recruiting members from the Korean community, most of whom were Methodists. He served both as preacher of his church and as leader of his political party.

It is debatable to this day whether the Korean community in Hawaii would have been as badly split had the Methodist Board of Missions, which was rigidly controlled by edicts from New England, not opposed Rhee's philosophy of education. That the Korean community in Hawaii was divided into two rival political parties was unfortunate; that the Korean community was divided into two rival churches was even more unfortunate.

The members of the Korean Christian Church exulted when their preacher, Syngman Rhee, returned from Washington, D.C., in 1919, where he had addressed a number of congressmen willing to listen to him on Korea's condition under colonial rule. The members of the church had further reason to gloat when Yongman Park was sentenced to deportation by the governor.

My mother had longed to return to the islands after her internment in prison. Upon her return, she thought she could resume her role as an activist for the cause of Korea's independence. But she found her role as a revolutionary suddenly changed. Two political parties had emerged, and the conflict between the two adversary leaders, Park and Rhee, had produced devastating results: the permanent split of the Korean community in Hawaii, the weakening of the independence movement, and the existence of two inimical Korean churches.

Both my parents remained Methodists, loyal to their church. They also continued to support Yongman Park by sending him funds regularly through party channels to Shanghai, where he was known to be training a military army. My mother especially favored Park's dream of expelling the Japanese in Korea by military force. She knew too well that a peaceful statement or an assertion of independence, like the event of March 1, 1919, was futile. As to Syngman Rhee's philosophy of education, which was the theme of his religious and political preaching, my mother could not fathom how it would bring about the liberation of Korea.

Outside of politics, there were other pressing matters in their lives that my parents could turn to. One of these that required their immediate attention was the matter of their daughter's schooling.

CHAPTER 5

A Scholarly Beginning

THE politics of Korea's independence were temporarily laid aside by my parents so they could attend to other matters. Meanwhile Syngman Rhee and his party prevailed, with stirring meetings at the Korean National Association headquarters on Miller Street. On Sundays the party men, dressed in their threadbare suits and straw hats, gathered together in large numbers and talked endlessly about independence and the latest news in the local Korean newspaper. Few if any of their wives invaded these meetings, although they were just as excited about the freedom movement.

My parents embarked on their dream of procuring a good education for me. Having already accepted the frustrating truth that she could not attend college, my mother wasted no time in trying to enroll me in a public school. The school term had begun in September. That I might be rejected worried my parents; it was November and perhaps too late for a child to register in a public school.

They turned for help to the man who lived next door. Mr. T. S. Lee, with his wife and five children, occupied one of the small houses identical to ours. He was tall for a Korean. Numerous freckles floated in his square face. His posture was always erect, as if his work demanded an upright, seemly appearance. He worked on the staff of the Nuuanu YMCA as a social worker. He assisted Koreans in the community, especially when an interpreter was needed. He promised my parents he would try his best to have me admitted to a school.

One morning, shortly after my seventh birthday, I held Mr.

Lee's hand as we entered Royal Grammar School on Queen Emma Street, two blocks away from where we lived. I trembled at the sight of the principal, a towering image in white. Cyril O. Smith wore a bushjacket, pants, and shoes—all in white. His short, bristly beard and close-cropped hair looked like patches of snow in a steep landscape. His voice boomed; he asked why I was registering so late in the year. When Mr. Lee explained the difficulty my mother and I had getting out of Yokohama, the principal raised one bushy white eyebrow and looked straight at me. I lowered my eyes. Then I heard him clear his throat and drop his hand on a desk bell. The secretary appeared from the next room.

"Follow the secretary," the principal said with authority. "She will fill out the registration forms."

Mr. Lee stood up and humbly offered, "Thank you very, very much, Mr. Smith."

With the registration forms in her hand, the secretary led us out of the two-story building to a bungalow, which housed the first graders. The room I was assigned to was bright and cheerful, with sunlight streaming in through the windows onto the tiny desks and seats lined up in rows. When Mr. Lee left me, I felt abandoned.

I knew I looked like a foreigner to the class. I had on a wool dress and shiny black shoes. All the other children were barefoot. They eyed me continually. How I longed to swing my legs freely as they did and be able to jump up noiselessly. I admired the way they trooped out of the room chatting easily with one another when the time came for recess.

The teacher put strange marks on the blackboard and the children recited the most unrecognizable sounds. "This is English. It is hard. But I must learn it," I kept reminding myself.

The next day I shed my shoes and socks and wore a cooler dress. Yet the uncomfortable feeling of being an oddity persisted.

I grumbled and cried everyday when I got home from school. In Korea I had been a star, loved and admired wherever I went. My mother was a great comfort. She sat patiently beside me in her *chi-ma* and *cho-gori* and helped me with my homework. She even *sounded* like the teacher; in her homeland she had learned to read primers in English. The lessons gradually became easier.

When she wistfully sighed one day, "I wish I were in your place in school," I felt guilty and vowed never to complain about school again.

As soon as I could speak their language, my classmates invited me to join them in games of hopscotch and tag. However, the children burst out laughing whenever I became excited and broke into a babble of rapid Korean. Then the old inferior feeling came over me again.

I had no way of knowing that I was fast learning to speak pidgin English. Once when a group of visitors to the school walked past my classmates and me on the playground, I decided to show off the English I had learned. In a loud voice I shouted to someone, "You no can do dat!" One of the visitors repeated, "Huh? 'You no can do dat'?" Believing I was being complimented for my fine English I beamed with pride.

Lunch recess was the hour I eagerly looked forward to. I ran to the cafeteria, which was in a separate bungalow. For five cents I could get a hot lunch, milk, and dessert. My favorites were macaroni and cheese, spaghetti and meat balls, and beef stew. When we became fourth graders, I knew our class would be called for cafeteria duty. Then we would help in the kitchen, serve lunch to the teachers and the students, get a free lunch, and go home early.

In contrast to the school lunches, the meals my mother prepared at home were not very tasty. She spent little time cooking. The kim chee invariably turned out to be either too salty or too bland. She apologized, "I guess I let the cabbage soak in salt water too long," or, "not long enough."

I'd forgotten that she had not stepped in a kitchen the previous three years and probably not in the eighteen years before she first came to Hawaii to marry my father. At twenty-six, Mother did not know how to cook nor could she sew. Both my parents believed that cooking and sewing were not important in a scholar's education. Therefore, I was kept from learning either skill.

"Study hard! Study hard!" were daily admonitions. An education was the most important reason for living, it seemed. I attended school all day. In the afternoon my Korean friends and I walked to the Methodist church on Fort Street to learn *Han-gul,* the Korean alphabet. The teacher told us, "You are fortunate because as immigrant children you all have a chance to be literate. Some children living in the rural areas of Korea do not have this opportunity to be educated."

I studied so hard that I anticipated the questions the teacher would ask. He chuckled one day, "Chung Sook, you're giving me the answers before I can finish asking the questions!" As long as I memorized each lesson, *Han-gul* was easy.

We pupils at Royal School were in awe of our teachers. They commanded respect. They looked dignified in their long dresses, which reached down to their ankles. By their names, such as Dunn, Kamaka, Cummings, and Rosa, I assumed they were either Hawaiian or haole, or a blend of both. When one of them stood on duty in the playground, I thought she looked like an elegantly dressed sentinel watching over us.

Later the teachers were caught in the "flapper age." As I moved to the upper grades, the dress styles of the teachers changed; their hemlines rose and strings of bright beads hung from each teacher's neck. Their teaching styles changed too, I thought, for they were impatient and in a hurry. It seemed as if there were so much more to learn than there was time for in a school year. So I studied even harder.

I remember two English teachers well. One was a Mrs. Marsland, who stressed grammar study. We were taught about nouns and verbs until we thought the world was made up of nothing else. If we looked hard enough, we were told, we could find adjectives and adverbs and prepositions. In her clear, young, strong voice, which sounded like continuous hammer blows, she pointed out the parts of speech.

Another teacher was a Miss Fujita, a short young lady with a round face—a recent graduate from the Normal School. She favored compositions. We sixth graders were constantly writing and receiving criticism from her. On one of my papers she noted, "You used the word *value* when you should have used *worth*." She admitted she had to read my paper over and over before she found the one mistake; she gave the paper an A— grade.

During my seventh year at Royal School I met two Korean girls from Los Angeles who impressed me. Our mothers were from the same province in Korea. Mary and Julie invited me often to their home.

For a long while they smiled with amusement at my bare feet, sunbrowned face, and casual dress and manners, whereas they felt uncomfortable going without shoes and socks even when they were at home. I was envious of their complexion—their fair skin and rosy cheeks. But what really attracted me to them was their lilting speech. It was so musical and different compared to the pidgin English my schoolmates spoke.

I tried to imitate their way of speaking. Instead of using the pidgin form like "Eh, dat look good!" I learned to say, "Oh, that looks nice!" Instead of "I no t'ink so," I'd say, "I don't think so."

My speech improved so noticeably after a few months of associating with them that the teachers selected me to be chairman of the school assemblies held each Friday, the day we entertained visitors to the school. I was seated with the honored guests on a semicircular dais, which was adorned with the American and Hawaiian flags, and with multihued hibiscus strung on long coconut sticks and planted in vases of sand. The hall was bright with the morning light pouring in through the open balcony windows and doors on the second floor. The students, sitting in groups by classes, stood up to sing the "Star-Spangled Banner" and bowed their heads for the invocation. As chairman, I led them in the responsive recitation of the Twenty-third Psalm. With a long prepared introduction I called on the speaker of the day, thanked him after his speech, and, last, asked everyone to stand and sing "Hawai'i Pono'i." Although the assembly program was formal and rigid each week, we children of Chinese, Japanese, Portuguese, and Korean immigrants sat very quiet and never complained. The speeches by the visitors, rendered in standard English, left us unmoved, and only the teachers laughed at the jokes.

My years at Royal Grammar School were satisfying with a few exceptions. During those years I knew that my parents could not afford to give me anything beyond the necessities.

I remember, for example, the many days after school when we children passed the small shops on Queen Emma Street on the way home. We eyed the array of delectable candies and cakes, crack-seed, sweet seed, sour seed, salt seed, abalone, dried shrimps, and small biscuits. The store owners did not mind our browsing around the tempting sweets stored in huge glass jars. For five cents one could get a whole bag of almost anything displayed. I yearned especially for the sticky, sweet crack-seed. But I could not afford it, and I did not get to share it when the rich kids bought some.

One day I told myself I *had* to have it. I could wait no longer. I skipped lunch that day and with the nickel saved I bought a whole bag of the juicy crack-seed after school. I was not about to share it with anyone. With the purchase in my school bag I hurried home and slipped away under the house. Crouched beneath the low house I sat on the dank, dark ground, and ate and ate to my heart's content. I was in heaven! On my tongue were the moist, sweet, slightly-tangy broken seeds, soaked in rich, brown, syrupy juice. I spit out the seeds only after I had sucked them clean.

Before I could finish the bagful, I felt a great thirst. That's when I heard my mother calling me to dinner.

After dinner, I suddenly felt ill. I went straight to bed. All night I was sick. Chills and sweat and nausea alternately swept over me. My whole body seemed to be on fire at times. Not until I had given up everything taken into my stomach that day did I finally fall asleep.

I did not graduate from Royal Grammar School. With only a year to go before I would finish the eighth grade and receive my diploma, my parents decided to move several miles away. For me, this meant changing schools.

Lincoln Junior High was just two blocks away from our new residence. Formerly a high school building, the old one-story concrete structure at the corner of Victoria and Beretania streets had on the front lawn a faded bluish-green statue of the president it was named after. Large letters, M C K I N L E Y, were inscribed above the dull, grey Ionic columns at the entrance. Mary and Julie attended the school and they urged me to join them.

Although Lincoln was a public school, it operated as a Standard English institution and only children able to speak and write what was considered "good English" by the special entrance exam testers were admitted. I passed the entrance exams.

I liked the school. Unlike Royal Grammar School, it offered interesting extracurricular activities. In the eighth grade I was on the staff of the school newspaper, and in the ninth grade I made the school debating team. There were about three hundred pupils in all, a hundred in each of the seventh, eighth, and ninth grades.

I graduated from Lincoln Junior High in 1930.

CHAPTER 6

The House on Pele Street

WE were a family that moved often. When my parents were expecting another child they decided to move to a bigger house about three blocks away on Magellan Avenue. This residence, although larger than the one on Iolani Avenue, pleased us for only a short time. The house was gloomy; dark brown varnished walls in each room contributed to the gloom. Moreover, the main rooms—the living room and the kitchen—never saw the sun even though they faced it every afternoon; a huge mango tree outside extended its massive branches, like the arms of a hulking giant, over the roof of the house.

The tree produced an overabundance of mangoes every year. We ate all we could, then we had to bag and distribute the excess to neighbors and friends—whoever was willing to take them off our hands. Still, there remained to be disposed of the fruit that was overripe or bird-pecked or worm-eaten. We put up with the annoyance of constant flies besides. How we shuddered whenever we heard mangoes falling at night when we were in bed!

A son, Young Mahn, was born while we lived there. My parents were proud, for a son would carry the family name. After two years we moved again, to a cottage on Pele Street. We reached this small charming house, which was just a few doors away, by taking a cemented walkway from the street into a court of seven houses. Young, short trees and green lawns gave the neighborhood a lush look. Bright zinnias bordered both sides of the walk up to our front steps.

The three bigger and newer houses in the court were occupied by noisy Portuguese families, while the four older, less-impressive ones were rented by quiet Asian families.

Our Pele Street house, built on a slight slope of the land, was bright and airy. The front veranda rose higher off the ground than the porch in the back; if we stood on our toes at the top of the front steps we could almost see the blue of the ocean. Corrugated tin roofs were common to all the cottages in the court.

My father liked the house because there was a makeshift room on the ground level built by the former tenant. "I'm going to fix the room under the house into a workshop," he announced at the dinner table one evening.

"What will you make, Abuji?" we asked.

He beamed with excitement. "You will see! I'm going to invent something."

"What? What did you say?" Mother spoke. Before she got a reply she chided, "You don't mean you're going to throw money away again to a lawyer?"

"Well, maybe I'll have to see a lawyer . . . ," he said with hesitation. But his eyes were shining. The under-the-house room suited short people like my father whose head just grazed the ceiling. He went on, "But first I'll have to do something to the floor. It's uneven. After I level it I'll build shelves, a long table, and—"

"But we should be saving money now. We have another baby coming. I told you that." Mother reminded him, gently touching her protruding body.

"I know that. Don't worry. This time I'll make money. I promise. You'll see."

"You didn't make money from your last invention."

"Oh, that—that was nothing much." He waved and dismissed the incident away.

My father's first invention was a small rubber attachment for the Singer Sewing Machine. He claimed the rubber attachment on the head of the machine would prevent marring of the board, which was folded against the head of the machine when the machine was not in use. Father had gone to a lawyer to obtain a U.S. patent for it. He was awarded a patent but apparently no sales resulted—no money was made.

Mother shook her head. "I happened to be away in Korea when you spent all that money you wasted. Now I'm here. Take my advice. Forget this foolishness."

He could be stubborn. In the years that followed whenever my father conceived an idea for a patent, which was often, it was like a dream that haunted and obsessed him until it became real. With his hands he molded ideas and fashioned them into something concrete.

We were happy living in the house on Pele Street. My second brother, Young Chul, was born there. Father worked at Coyne Furniture Company, and he rose rapidly from the apprentice stage of upholsterer. He told us he talked with wealthy customers of the store when they stopped by at the warehouse and sought his advice on how to reupholster their furniture.

After his workday at Coyne Furniture he came home and headed straight for the room under the house to engage in his favorite pastime. At first the workshop looked neat, with smoothed floor, tools on shelves, a sturdy work table planed and polished, and a single lightbulb hanging suspended on a wire from the ceiling. The latticed-wood walls let in air as well as the sun's fading rays.

Later, when large sheets of metal were delivered to the house, the workshop grew chaotic with litter. Basically my father was not a tidy person, while my mother lived by a traditional sense of order and sanity. He left orders for us not to touch or move any of the patterns and cuttings of paper or metal lying on the table and the floor. Mother grumbled and mumbled at the mess he left behind, "How can he be so messy!"

Months went by. Although we heard hammering and tinkering in the workshop everyday we forgot about the new invention. However, one day Father surprised us. He announced that he was ready for a preview showing of his latest creation. Late in the afternoon he called the entire family to the kitchen. He stood in front of the kerosene stove.

The stove, with three tall, blue, cylindrical chimneys, was fed by a gallon of kerosene, which was inverted on the side of the stove; the kerosene flowed into a pipe that ran horizontally beneath the tall chimneys.

Father held a strange-looking iron plate with hammered-up edges and a large hole in the center. It looked crude. He fitted the iron plate on top of one of the chimneys so that the plate rested securely on the chimney yet allowed the flame to pass through the hole.

Then he took a pot of rice, which had been washed and was soaking in water, and put it on the grill directly above the chimney with the new invention on it. He raised the chimney at the bottom, next to the flue, and lit the circular wick inside the chimney.

"No one must touch the pot till I say so," Father warned. Mother looked skeptical. I wondered what we were to wait for. Soon we heard bubbling sounds from the pot. Mother's hand quickly reached over to lift the pot cover to prevent the liquid from boiling over.

Father caught her hand. "No! No! Don't touch it!" he cried. "Just wait!"

The liquid in the rice pot kept boiling and gurgling. Another minute passed before he turned down the flame. We noticed the gooey liquid had flowed over the pot into the iron plate.

Father turned to us, his eyes glowing with pride and triumph. "See! No need to stand and watch over the rice cooking anymore. No more accidents. No sticky water to clean off the sides of a chimney and the bottom of the stove. No more mess. Simply pick up the plate after cooking and wash it."

Mother edged closer to the stove. She nodded slowly with appreciation and approval. "Yobo, that's a good idea. I think my friends Mrs. Kim and Mrs. Lee will want one of these."

He replied, "Of course, they will. Don't you think every woman will want one? Isn't this a wonderful invention?" Mother nodded her head in agreement.

Our family as well as all the neighbors in the court knew what to expect as soon as my father got home from work each day. We became accustomed to the sounds of cutting, pounding, and banging in the shop.

But one day a huge, heavy, mechanical contraption was delivered and installed in the workshop. The neighbors then were subjected to horrendous noises from sundown to midnight. First, there was high-pitched squealing and grinding, followed by a series of loud, quivering crunches, and finally a shattering boom! A heavy cylindrical hole-puncher had descended on a stack of metal squares and cut a hole clean through the stack.

Mr. Chun, who lived across from us, said the first time he heard the boom he thought it was the firing of a cannon ball. His wife remarked, "I shuddered. I thought your house was being torn apart!" Other neighbors complained they couldn't fall asleep with so much noise at night, but they also said they were getting used to it.

Father called his invention by a simple name: chimney plate. It looked simple in construction but it was not easy to make. For the first samples, which he laboriously made by hand, he used heavy shears, pliers, hammer, and chisel. He found the thick sheetmetal unrelenting and difficult to slice in curves. He realized he would never make enough money manufacturing the invention by hand, not enough even to cover expenses. He did not wish to invest any more money for fear of Mother's objections. But he rationalized he had to spend a little more to make any money at all.

Meanwhile his attorney was encountering trouble in procuring a patent. My father expressed a theory as to why the process was taking so long: "Maybe those patent judges in Washington, D.C., don't cook rice."

Finally the patent on the chimney plate was granted. Anyone who could read English would have noted that the patent was awarded primarily for the innovative idea of a *heat reflector*.

U.S. Patent No. 1,499,226, issued June 24, 1924 is described as follows:

> The principal object of this invention is to provide a cheap and efficient device, which will catch the heat rising from a flame

having hot spots and dissipating the heat so that it is evenly distributed over a given area . . .

Another object is to provide a device which at the same time will act as a receptacle for the purpose of receiving any liquid which may be discharged from the receptacle placed thereon, such as a boiling over of the contents of the receptacle . . .

My father enjoyed steady sales of his new invention. Manufacturing the chimney plates was a slow process; working with metal was difficult with the limited machinery he had. But he was gratified that the Korean, Chinese, Japanese, and Portuguese, who ate rice everyday, bought the product.

Sundays were special days for all the immigrant families living in our Pele Street court. Early in the morning I saw the Portuguese families leaving for mass. They were dressed in their finery—the girls and their mothers in bright pink, blue, or printed dresses and stylish hats; the boys and their fathers in trim suits and felt hats. Each family walked together to the cathedral. Although the parents yelled and scolded their children during the week, on Sundays they were all quiet and amiable. The two Japanese families in the court did not make a weekly ritual of going to church. I heard they had shrines built in their homes, so they held their own services.

Our family walked together to our Methodist church on Fort Street. We wore our best clothes, although they did not compare with the showy, splendid dress of the Portuguese.

The congregation of over a hundred members at our church was like a large, intimate clan of relatives; we knew all the families by name. The men in their worn suits entered the sanctuary through the door on the left and sat in the pews on the left, while the women in their native dress and their children in homemade Western clothes entered through the door on the right and occupied the center and right pews.

Parishioners were most happy to see each other, but they did not express their pleasure openly. They followed a dignified custom they had brought from their country: they responded to greetings with utmost humility. When asked, "How are you?" the appropriate answer was "Oh, so so," or "Not much better than last week," or "All right, I guess." These responses belied the feelings of the women, especially, who were usually full of joy.

When the church service was over, everyone hurried home for a quick lunch—no one lived too far away—then returned for club meetings and socials. The men retired in small groups and discussed Korean politics. The women put their energies into the mission of the Methodist Ladies' Aid Society—keeping track of the sick or unemployed or troubled among its members.

We children returned with our parents to the church, too. We had the whole Sunday afternoon to play games or just sit and chat with one another until our parents were ready to go home.

Later my father began dropping from church attendance. This upset my mother. She knew he favored his workshop over Sunday worship. Before long he stopped going to church altogether. She begged him to keep up the appearance of family unity. She began worrying about his soul. She admonished, "You know, you're worshipping the *akma!* You're not supposed to work on the Sabbath." I knew the *akma* was the devil.

She deplored his excuses: "I can't make the chimney plates fast enough. If I don't hurry, the customers will cancel their orders. Sunday is the only time I have to catch up."

"But I don't want to see you lose your soul!"

The weekends became turbulent days in our home. Mother threw accusations at Father, then, filled with remorse, she begged him to consider her advice. He countered with defenses and reproval of all religious matters. Invariably the arguments ended when he declared he had to prove he could make money from this invention because he had promised her he would.

What stamina he exhibited standing on his feet from five o'clock in the morning until late Sunday night. Sometimes I heard him humming happily, his stubby fingers shaping and reshaping each metal plate.

The women's haggling over the price of the chimney plates

annoyed him. One cried, "For this small piece tin, you charge me one dollar! Do you know what I can buy with one dollar? Four pounds meat!" Another complained, "I think you're cheating us. What're you going to do with all the money you make?" When a woman purchased more than one plate at a time she made it known she was doing him a great favor.

Meanwhile, all was going well with his job as an upholsterer. Perhaps too well. He was known in the trade as a first-rate upholsterer. Bailey Furniture Company, the most prestigious home furnishings shop in Honolulu and a competitor of Coyne Furniture, lured my father away to their shop by offering him wages and benefits he could not refuse. Then another tempting offer came to him from a man who was opening a new business in town. The man's name was Calistro.

"Who is this Calistro?" my mother asked. "Where does he come from?"

"I don't know. I never heard of him before. He says he'll open the biggest furniture store in Hawaii. He promises me I'll be the highest-paid upholsterer in town."

Calistro, a flamboyant entrepreneur, opened his retail showroom on the corner of Alakea and Beretania streets. His store was packed with expensive furniture and glittering decorative objects.

As the months passed, my father grew more and more worried for there were so few reupholstery jobs. He was standing idle much of the time in the warehouse.

The Calistro firm folded about a year after it opened. The year was 1928.

A terrible, depressing gloom settled over our house after Father lost his job. The gloom grew worse each day. I found it almost unbearable to stay in the house. Father sat stolid in a chair all day without stirring from it. He seemed to have lost interest even in his once-favorite pastime; the door under the house remained shut.

The news of his doom traveled fast to neighbors and friends, and to his former employers Bailey and Coyne as well. The companies sent letters by mail and by messenger, asking him to return to them. But he did not respond to the letters. He just sat and brooded day after day, week after week.

When I came home from school one day I found my father's chair empty. From that day he began taking short trips out of the house. The next week I heard the workshop downstairs humming at a feverish pitch. I wondered whether my father was going to do nothing but make chimney plates.

One afternoon I found my mother looking very solemn. What had happened? What was going to happen? Why did she look so strange?

Then I heard the big news. "Your father will never go back to work for either Coyne or Bailey. He can't. He feels he has 'lost face.' "

A minute later she said, "He claims there is only one thing left for him to do. He will open his own upholstery business."

CHAPTER 7

Starting Anew

In 1928 my father started his own business, and soon he found himself sailing right into the Great Depression. He depended on the *Nippu Jiji,* a Japanese daily he subscribed to, for coverage of world news and information on the state of the economy. The paper was small and the coverage scanty. Japanese, he could read; Korean, he could read and write; but English, he could neither read nor write. To communicate with others, he relied on the common, spoken pidgin English. He was familiar with the language of his trade, which he had picked up at Coyne and Bailey furniture stores. His only assets as a new businessman seemed to be a talent for upholstering and a dogged determination to succeed.

Honolulu was a sprawling, growing city with electric trolley cars and black Ford Model A automobiles on its roads. Big *kamaaina* businesses were established on King Street, the main street, and on Bishop, Merchant, and Fort streets.

My father found a small shop for rent on Nuuanu Street. The shop, which was between a candy store and an herb grocer, measured twenty feet wide by twenty-five feet deep. Soon upholstery supplies filled the shop: rolls of cotton padding and bolts of fabrics, boxes of tacks and screws, also spring forms for chairs and couches. There were also a couple of carpenters' horses upon which to mount chairs and sofas. Other items included a second-hand desk and two chairs, and a used power sewing machine. For delivery, a small used truck was purchased.

One day our family went down to visit Father at the shop. Mother looked impressed and a little nervous. I was filled with

pride. Every night I had heard my parents discussing the excit-
ing new enterprise. I heard Mother, who was the banker and
controller of finances, warn again and again, "Yobo, you're
spending too much too fast. Be careful. Pretty soon we'll have
no money left in our savings!"

We came upon Father with his only employee, Mr. Ordway,
surveying the crowded shop and shaking their heads. Ordway, a
tall, lean Englishman with a high nose, sunken cheeks, and grey
hair, suffered from a hacking cough. He rolled his cigarettes and
smoked them one after another. I never learned where he came
from except that he had worked with my father and had lost his
job at Calistro's at the same time. He was an old, wrinkled man
with no wife to go home to.

Fortunately Ordway could read and write English, and his
speech was soft and gracious, even witty at times. He gave won-
derful support to my father's ideas. They made a pair, laughing
and joking. "You know, Kwon, you're a smart man. A little
crazy, maybe, but smart," he jested.

I don't know who thought up the name of the shop but they
agreed to call it King Furniture Co., because, they said, they
were going to be the best in the field. A long sign, with bold,
black letters, was put up the day before the official opening.
How hard they had worked, day and night, to be ready for
business.

They had hurried only to wait: wait for business, for custom-
ers to walk in, for clients to call. The black desk phone with the
easy-to-remember number 2468 was silent. Korean friends of
the family could not afford upholstered furniture. Apparently
no one in Honolulu was interested in the reupholstering services
my father offered.

When Father came home in the evenings we knew how he felt
by his dejected appearance. "We had no business again today,"
he'd mutter, grinding his teeth and staring in space. My brothers
did not seem affected but I felt depressed. What would happen
to us if Father had no work?

But a turn of events occurred as a result of Ordway's brilliant
suggestion. "Why don't I call some of the rich people in this

town—you know—the ones that used to drop by at Coyne and Bailey? Maybe they don't know yet that you're on your own, Kwon. How would they know if no one tells them?

"You think—?"

"Yes! We can't go on doing nothing like this every day. Let's call them."

So Ordway contacted the Cookes, the Dillinghams, the Damons, and the Judds, among others. Gracious and gentle, he tried to persuade them to try the services of King Furniture Co. He promised they would find the lowest prices in town for the finest work.

Since Ordway could not operate the truck and my father could not speak proper English, it was necessary to close the shop and both of them go on initial calls to the homes of clients to quote estimates. Then when the "lady" (as a client was usually referred to) reached a decision, again the two men got into the truck to pick up the furniture to be reupholstered.

It wasn't long before sleek, chauffered limousines were driving up to my father's small place of business. Fashionably dressed women stepped out of the cars and entered the shop. The Japanese chauffeur in a black cap and grey suit followed the lady with bolts of beautiful expensive fabrics. The lady selected the gimp or cord trimmings from an array that my father stocked for the edges of their antique furniture, and she asked for and made suggestions.

A period of steady business followed, supplying work for Ordway and my father. But new problems arose. They found even if they worked day and night the business was not yielding a profit. Father brought home at night most of the cushions for the finishing touches; he and Mother used long or curved needles to sew the seams after the cushions had been filled at the shop. Money was short. I heard that the savings at the bank had dwindled to almost nothing. Father regretted he couldn't find the time to engage in earning extra cash by making more chimney plates.

According to him, the most pressing problem was the cramped quarters. "I must do something about that soon," he declared with frustration. "There's just not enough room in the shop to move around. We have to push this and push that to make room to get any work done."

He continued to vent his frustration. It seemed he had opened the gates once he started naming his problems, and the concerns of his mind came rushing forth. "I can't be the truck driver. That's a delivery boy's job. I must stay in and do the work." Then he almost shouted, "I've got to find a bigger place and I've got to hire a delivery boy!"

Rainy weather brought problems. Most of the stores on Nuuanu Street had no front doors—only outer front walls that could be folded manually, like an accordion, and pushed to one side. The contents of the store were subjected to the dust of the street as well as the fine, misty rain that swept down the valley daily from the Pali. When heavy rains fell and gusty winds raged on Nuuanu, the "door" had to be shut. The interior then became a hot, suffocating place, tools and supplies and furniture piled up on top of the other. There was a narrow back door which opened almost smack into the wall of the next building, providing little if any ventilation.

Rain, wind, and dust, moreover, threatened stains and discolorations on the customers' beautiful damasks and linens. In those days fabrics were not treated for resistance to water and dirt. A fine drizzle in Nuuanu was a daily hazard to the contents of the shop.

While my father was struggling with his business, life for us at home on Pele Street went on as usual, except for the sewing lessons my mother was taking. Some of her friends were adept as tailors, a trade they were forced to learn as tailors' wives. The fact was, to save money, all the Korean women were helping each other learn to sew dresses and shirts and pants for their families. They gradually gave up their own *chi-ma* and *cho-gori* for the American-style dress.

One Sunday afternoon as I was returning home after visiting a friend, I bumped into my father, who was leaving the house in what seemed a great hurry.

"Where are you going?" I asked.

"Out! Out!" he cried. "There's too much noise there!" He pointed to our house. "Those women in there—they drive me crazy!" He was gone before I could ask where he was headed.

I walked toward the house. I could hear women's voices, laughing and chatting. I remembered the Youngnam Puin Hoe ladies were holding their meeting at our house that day. When I entered the living room I came upon such a crescendo of high-pitched and excited voices that I raised my hands to cover my ears. Why was everyone talking at once, I wondered.

I counted fifteen women sitting on the floor in a circle, some wearing the *chi-ma* and *cho-gori,* others in plain cotton American-style dresses. Before them, on the floor, was an array of food in large pans and bowls and baskets. The fare looked familiar but the quantities surprised me.

One of the ladies glancing up saw me and exclaimed, "Why, look who's here. It's Chung Sook!" Then a shrill chorus echoed, "It's Chung Sook."

Mrs. Han remarked, "Oh, my, Chung Sook, you're so skinny. Come here and eat with us. We must fatten you." I was offended by the way she invited me although I was used to being labelled thin.

Piled up high in an oversized basket were long leaves of lettuce, farm fresh and glistening with water. Next to the basket was a huge tub of steaming white rice. Mrs. Choi, a quiet and efficient-looking lady, picked up the wooden *chu-gae,* which was a much larger version of our own rice server, and filled a bowl with the rice. Then she picked up another bowl and ladled *tubu-chige* from a pot. The *tubu-chige* was one of my favorite dishes—white cubes of *tubu* floating in a delicious spicy broth, with chunks of meat and peppery pickled cabbage and sliced green onion. I noticed many chopsticks flitting in and out of the gallon jar of kim chee, the turnips and cabbage in it bathed in a red pepper sauce. There were dark fish preserves in *kan-jang* and finely shredded vegetables marinated in a pinkish pepper sauce.

Mrs. Lee, a fat woman, demanded my attention. "Chung

Sook, watch me." She picked up two or three large leaves of lettuce and shook the excess water from them. "You make a bed with this lettuce, then put a mound of rice in it, and a piece of fish, a couple of pieces of kim chee, and last a big dab of *ko-chu-jang* (a thick, red, hot, chili pepper paste) on top. Be sure you fold the leaves to make a ball." She couldn't get the whole concoction into her mouth at once, so she nibbled around the edges first. When she finally pushed the remainder in, her cheeks bulged as she munched.

The gay chattering continued unabated although everyone seemed to be consuming food. Suddenly a burst of laughter from one corner of the room drew attention to three or four women who were laughing so hard that they held their hands up to their faces to keep food from falling out of their mouths.

"What's so funny?" someone asked.

A young woman named Soon Young, her pretty face flushed, her black hair bunned in the back, began relating in spurts and giggles: "We were just talking about Silla Eun—you know—that prim and proper lady from Seoul." Soon Young then rose to her knees, straightened her rumpled purple *chi-ma,* and began mimicking the overly mannered Silla. Turning her head from side to side, pursing her lips, and in a high, affected tone Soon Young murmured, "Oh, is that so? I did not know that. Ex-cuse me, please." The exaggerated twisting movements imitating a refined lady from the capital of Korea brought guffaws and slapping of thighs from the audience. Before sitting down, the mimicker said, "Silla must think we from Kyungsangdo are so crude and loud. Ha! Ha! Ha!"

It was growing dark outside and almost all the food was gone. Mother's friends picked up the dishes and serving receptacles and crowded into the kitchen. The room reverberated with happy voices. These women like noise and gaiety, I thought, shaking my head.

The spring days were growing warmer and the zinnias in the yard looked brighter and prettier than ever. There was a peace and loveliness in the Pele Street court that I suddenly appreciated. In the afternoon after school the girls in the neighborhood and I practiced high kicks and splits, as if we were dancers, or turned cartwheels, like clowns, spinning from one neighbor's lawn to the next. Sometimes we sat under a cherry or a mango tree and chatted, or lay on the cool grass and sang all the songs we knew. I don't know why I felt so happy. Perhaps it was because I had finally adjusted to school life and no one looked on me any longer as a foreigner.

One evening at dinner I received a terrible jolt. Mother announced we were moving again.

"Where to? Why?" I cried. I couldn't believe what I heard. There couldn't be a better place to live than on Pele Street, I thought.

"Will I have to change schools?" my brother Young Mahn asked.

"I guess so," Mother replied drily.

"Where're we moving to?" I demanded. I looked to Father; his eyes were on his food. Anger was building up in me. "I want to know where we're moving to!"

Mother spoke in a voice with no feeling. "We're moving to a store."

Young Mahn laughed. "How can we live in a store? Will all the people passing by see us eating and sleeping?"

"No. We'll be living above the store, on the second floor."

I objected. "Omoni, I don't want to move. I want to live right here!"

All of a sudden Father's voice thundered. "You listen to your mother!" His eyes were flashing. He ordered, "You listen to her. Stop this complaining!"

I bowed my head. I felt I had been struck. No one said anything more during the rest of the meal.

The next day after school I saw my mother in the bedroom, sorting and packing clothes into boxes. I asked if she needed help. She did not answer. I stood at the door and waited.

After a while she sat down on the bed, presumably to rest. She beckoned me.

"Chung Sook, your father says he must move his shop to a

bigger place. He has looked and looked all over the city. The only suitable place he's found is this old building—in fact, a set of buildings. We can live there, too. There's so much room. It looks like three families lived there once.

"It's a huge place, too big for our business. But all the other rental spaces your father saw were too expensive or too small for his purposes."

"But can't we stay here?"

"I'd like to. Just as much as you do." She looked weary and a little sad. "But we can't afford to. Your father cannot pay the rents for both places. Remember that."

Mother patted me. "Be good. Try not to upset your father."

Above, The author's mother, Hee Kyung Lee, as an 18-year-old picture bride in 1912. *Left,* The author's father, Do In Kwon, at age 25 in 1914.

The Korean Methodist Church on Punchbowl Street in 1915. The author and her mother are in the front row, tenth seat from right.

Syngman Rhee in 1940, before he became the first president of the Republic of Korea after WWII.

Yongman Park, as he appeared in approximately 1913.

The traditional see-saw jumping game, *nul-dwi-gi,* as played in Korea.

Hee Kyung Lee Kwon at age 26. She is
wearing the traditional *chi-ma* and *cho-gori*.

Hee Kyung Lee Kwon (left) in Korean
revolutionary's uniform in 1918.

Hee Kyung Lee Kwon (center) with friends in a studio portrait
taken in 1924.

The author's mother (age 31) and father (age 37) relaxing in 1925.

The author (second row, center) and her 7th grade class at Royal School in 1927.

Korean bride and groom (here, the author's uncle) in traditional wedding dress, approximately 1930.

Popular singer from Korea with the author's mother and her friends on the steps of Roosevelt High School, approximately 1936.

The author and her mother at the author's graduation from the University of Hawaii in 1937.

Do In Kwon, prior to leaving on a
business trip to Japan in 1940.

The author's father and mother
outside of their factory in 1946.

Hee Kyung Lee Kwon (seated first chair on right) seving as a Red Cross
volunteer in 1945.

Hee Kyung Lee Kwon at age 53 in 1947.

The author's daughter, Merphil, in 1947. She is wearing the *chi-ma* and *cho-gori,* styled for little girls.

The author and her father in 1958, preparing to leave Hawaii via Pan American airlines for a business trip.

The author and her children, Merphil and Garet, in 1955.

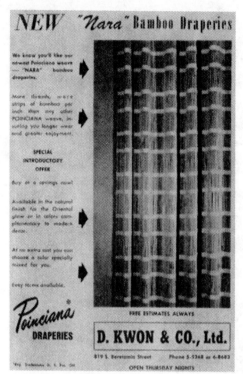

An advertisement for one of the many styles of Poinciana Draperies produced by D. Kwon & Co.

The author visiting the U.S. Patent and Trademark Office in Crystal City, Virginia, in 1982.

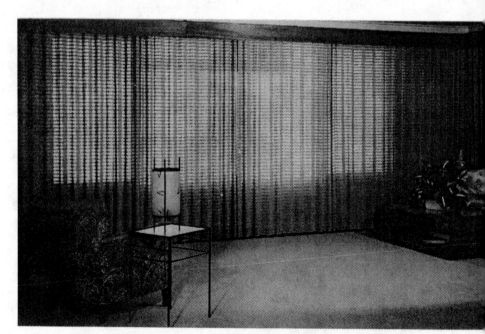

Installed Poinciana Draperies at the author's home in 1952.

CHAPTER 8

Growing Up in a Factory

As WE packed our belongings preparing to move, I wished we could pack the pleasures and delights of living in the Pele Street court. I loved our sunny and airy house, the flowers and the fruit trees in the front yard. I would miss our neighbors, especially the girls my age who played with me.

And I suddenly felt a rush of warmth I hadn't felt before for the noisy Portuguese family living next door to us. When the three lively boys were reprimanded by their bellicose mother, we could hear her—whether she was outside or in: "Antone, Manuel, Joe, you stop throwing things at each other!" Mrs. Gomez's two aims in life were to keep her house spotless and her children tractable, and her aims were often in conflict. All day she carried a rag in her hand. Once she invited me to view her collection of figurines and dolls set on snow-white doilies, on shelves and tables and chests, even on the ledges high up next to the ceiling. Her boys had to walk around the dolls and figurines with caution.

Everyday the three Portuguese families in the court diligently hosed their red-cement front porches and steps. They took great pride in keeping their homes inside and out neat and presentable at all times.

Across from us lived Mrs. Lyu and her children, who kept very quiet, as if in shame. Mr. Lyu, a small, aloof man, was a heavy drinker. Sometimes he caused a commotion when he raised his voice and beat his wife and two young sons. Occasionally I saw Mrs. Lyu hanging her laundry on the line or working in her garden. She moved slowly, usually with her head bowed and her shoulders stooped. The day she came home from a visit to the doctor, she looked grave. She said he had told her, "You're not sick. You worry too much. If you want to feel well, you should always have something pleasant to look forward to." When I mentioned the fun my mother had with her Youngnam Puin Hoe friends, Mrs. Lyu's eyes brightened. I hoped she would join them. I knew I would miss her.

Finally the day arrived for us to move. The shop and apartment were located on Beretania Street, opposite the town water pumping station. The store was one in a row of shops in a dilapidated two-story building. To get to our living quarters we had to go through the store; there was no other way because all the shops shared common walls.

I noticed the long sign, King Furniture Co., was already up in front. Compared to my father's last place of business this store was enormous, looking almost bare even with the heavy power sewing machine, an oversized work table, some customers' furniture to be reupholstered, and the workmen's horses. In a corner of this barnlike room was the office, consisting merely of a battered roll-top desk, chair, telephone, and adding machine. The front wall of the store measured at least three times that of the former Nuuanu shop. The upper half of this wall was made up of thick glass in twelve-inch squares. When new, the glass must have looked shiny and expensive but now it was dingy and discolored.

The aged glass squares and the one small window in the back admitted hardly enough light for the large showroom and work area. Only a few electric bulbs hung from the ends of wires from the ceiling. On dark, cloudy days, the shadows in the corners of the store would frighten me, for the white muslin-covered chairs and sofas, stripped of their outer covering, looked like phantoms floating in space.

We did not own much in the way of household goods. Yet Mother and I were exhausted from carrying cloth bundles filled with bedding and clothing, kitchenware, and books from the truck to the apartment. Father, however, no matter how many boxes he carried, seemed to have unlimited energy. Again and again he exclaimed, "This place is so good! So much room for everybody!" With our arms loaded we climbed the rickety stairs to the second floor while my brothers spent a good part of the sunny day having fun on the stairs, which squealed whenever they stepped on a loose, termite-eaten board.

"I don't like it here at all," I complained with disdain. The kitchen had to double for a living, dining, and study room. Mother said nothing; I was longing to be back in the house on Pele Street, but she was probably thinking of her gracious, comfortable home in Taegu. There were no curtains or shades anywhere in the apartment. We looked for closets and found none; we had to wait for Father to put up narrow shelves with hooks under them to hang our clothes.

The four bedrooms were oddly arranged. It seemed somebody had taken one large room and divided it in half, then the two in half again. As a result we were obliged to walk through one bedroom to get to the next.

It rained hard that first night in our new home. The pelting sounds of the rain on the tin roof seemed much louder and harsher than I'd ever heard on Pele Street.

The next day I explored the premises and was amazed at the sheer size of the property. At the foot of our rickety stairs was an area of worn, cracked cement, about fifteen feet square. On one side of this square, directly behind the main store space, was a separate building, housing a cavernous carpenter shop, and above it another apartment. Across from the staircase, on the other side of the square, was a small lavatory; this room was kept scrupulously clean because there was in it, besides the toilet, something left behind by the former tenant that Mother prized dearly—a wooden *furo*. This rectangular box made of wood was about twenty-eight inches deep and slippery on the inside. A crackling fire in the woodstove alongside it heated water almost to the boiling point.

From the second night we moved there and every night thereafter my mother sat in the tub, immersed in almost-scalding water, with only her head showing. My father refused to use the *furo*, for he said it took too long to bathe in it. On our mother's insistence, once a week after my brothers and I scrubbed ourselves, we soaked ourselves in the *furo*.

Instead of his business improving at the new location, my father said he found it harder than ever to make money. He hired a young Korean boy to make deliveries and to drive Ordway to clients' homes to give estimates on jobs. My father dreaded the first day of each month when the rent and wages had to be paid. Food could be purchased only with cash, and the last days of each month saw little on our table. The calendar got to be something we all kept our eyes on so that we knew when to expect Father to go into his monthly act of agonizing and despairing. "Damn, damn, damn," he'd cry, "where in hell will I get the money to—to—"

Poor Mother. Living on the premises of the business, she was unable to escape his misery and curses. She regretted the day she had generously offered to "give a hand," because she was trapped into working full time, doing everything except the carpentering and the painting. She was the seamstress. She operated the awesome power sewing machine that roared like many misaligned wheels rotating in a confined space; the needle in this fast sewing machine could make deep stitches in almost anything, including your finger if you weren't careful. Mother also learned to take phone messages in her broken English, and she was the overseer of the employees when Father went out on calls.

Somehow our business survived the first difficult months at the new shop. The spaciousness of the facilities inspired my father to expand his services. He transformed the shop into a factory, starting with remodeling the old furniture of customers —changing their appearance and structure from the typical swollen-looking, old-fashioned pieces to furniture with sleek, trim lines.

Philippine mahogany, the fine-grained hardwood, was introduced for "modern" tables with straight legs and square-edged tops. This mahogany, when sanded and polished, was light in color and silken to the touch. Eventually my father built custom-ordered furniture for bedrooms, dining rooms, and lanais.

New electrical machines were purchased to hasten production. The bandsaw whining, the constant hammering, and the spray painting filled the air with a cacophony of sounds.

More new employees were hired and trained. Yin Hong and Jimmie, the young upholstery apprentices, soon learned to imitate my father by throwing handfuls of tacks into their mouths, bringing the magnet end of their hammers to their lips, and tacking rhythmically away. Yin Hong was meticulous and worked slowly. My father often praised him for the beautiful work he did. Jimmie, on the other hand, was quick in temperament and style, his mouth always full of tacks, his hammer continually moving. Sometimes he was asked to peel off and retack the covering of a chair because the work did not have "a finished look." Yet I was surprised when I heard Father say to Mother he favored Jimmie over Yin Hong because "with supervision and practice, Jimmie will work faster and make more money for the company."

Our life changed with the addition of a new member to the family, a girl named Chung Hee. When she was born, two or three women from the Korean Methodist Church came to cook for us as well as do the washing. After a month my mother was able to work at the shop again.

Soon after my sister's birth my parents announced we were moving again. I envisioned a house with a lawn and flowers. But I was disappointed. We were moving to the apartment next door, the one above the carpenter shop. My father reasoned he could be having lunch and be watching the store from the other apartment, which was directly behind the store. The fact that there was a separate living room in that apartment pleased me. But the kitchen was an embarrassment. It had no door, no glass in the windows; in fact, the windows were only mesh screens above the sink and counter. When it rained, the cook got wet as well as the kitchen itself. But the advantage was the cook could check any activity going on in the store, including any customer walking in.

What an exciting day it was when a customer placed a really big order! A man with blondish hair walked into the store and admired a bedroom set made of Philippine mahogany. He was delighted with the smooth sliding of the drawers. He lavished praise on the unusual vanity dressing table. He did not mention a wife or family or where he lived. He had brought with him on a truck some old furniture which he wished to have reupholstered. There was a casualness about this man that made my father believe he was an easy customer to please. The order amounted to a total of four hundred dollars and the customer agreed to pay in full when he came by to pick up all the furniture upon completion of the job.

The next few weeks saw feverish activity in the factory. My parents talked at night about how many bills they could pay with the four hundred dollars.

How proud the employees were when the blond customer walked in some weeks later and approved of what he saw of his order. He wrote a check for the full amount due. Then he asked for help in loading all the pieces of furniture onto the truck he had brought. With a handshake and a smile he drove off.

The next day my father learned the check was worthless. An officer at the Bank of Hawaii advised there was no account in the name scrawled on the check. Dismayed beyond words, my father staggered back to the shop.

The devastating loss in terms of labor, materials, and time proved a bitter lesson in how to run a business. None of his customers' checks had been bad before this.

Then, a few weeks after the incident, an extremely well-dressed man came by taxi to the store. When he said he was from Hollywood and wished to place an order, my father's resistance antennae went up. The gentleman, who gave his name as Edwin B. Willis, stated he had been a guest at a home at Diamond Head, where he had seen just the kind of tropical furniture he had been looking for. Would my father build a complete rattan set for a room? And ship the set to his studio in Hollywood? Mr. Willis added he was staying at the Royal Hawaiian Hotel.

That evening I heard my father laugh as he related to Mother that haoles were such cunning people. "This crazy fellow," Father said, "thinks I will be so stupid as to make all this furniture for him, then *ship* it to California! Ha!"

Mother was less suspicious of the customer whose order for nine hundred dollars' worth of rattan-trimmed furniture could help cover a lot of bills. She suggested, "Why don't you ask Mr. Willis to pay for the order in advance?"

A week later the gentleman from Hollywood dropped in the store again, and again he was impeccably dressed in a perfect-fitting suit, polished shoes, and a Panama hat. He announced he was leaving Honolulu the next day. He wished to verify his order and give the shipping address.

My father nervously cleared his throat. Meekly he said, "Mr. Willis, will you please pay for the job now before I start?"

Mr. Willis quickly responded. "Oh, when I get back I will have MGM send you a purchase order." Then he was gone.

What to do with this order? Neither my parents nor anyone we knew had heard of MGM. Father's inclination was to forget the visit of this man from Hollywood. But Mother, who had observed the man and believed him, pressed with "Let's go ahead and fill the order. I think the man is honest."

A few days later my father called me. "Chung Sook, I want you to write a letter for me. To Mr. Willis in California." On ruled composition paper I used in school (I was in the seventh grade) I wrote in longhand to Mr. Willis at Metro-Goldwyn-Mayer Studios, Culver City, California, asking him about some detail in the design of the rattan set he had ordered.

The reply came promptly, with the assurance that a purchase order was being processed.

Eventually, with that official document in hand, my father risked making up the order. It wasn't until many, many years later, during the revival of the MGM Classics of the Twenties and Thirties, that I noted among the screen credits, in film after film, the name of Edwin B. Willis, Set Designer. His name always followed that of the well-known Cedric B. Gibbons, Art Director.

Looking out from the apartment we had moved to I could see the cottages of our neighbors. I watched with interest from my bedroom the Japanese neighbors on that side of the house when they took their daily community baths. In a narrow, fenced-in portion of their property behind their shops the children bathed first in late afternoon. The bathers crouched and chit-chatted around a metal tub about thirty inches in diameter, which contained clean, hot water. I saw the youngsters dip little pails into the community tub and pour water over their bodies to rinse off the soaping. Often a mother or an aunt, adding more hot water to the tub, scolded the children for raising their voices and playing games instead of concentrating on their bath.

In the evening when it was the adults' turn to bathe, the tall papaya trees growing alongside the high fence separating their property from ours provided enough of a screen to make it difficult for me to distinguish their bodies from my window. But on moonlit nights I could see and, somehow, hear better. Sometimes I heard three or four women huddled over the tub, their voices low and muted. At other times I was sure I saw both men and women, naked, squatting side by side, their feet in heavy Japanese wooden *geta,* their whispers a blend of high and low conversational tones. When I heard repeated splashing sounds, I knew the bath ritual was nearly over.

The neighbors on the other side of our apartment were shopkeepers with no apartments above or behind their places of business.

Around the corner, facing a side street, was the large house in which our rich landlord lived. His property ran all the way back to our factory. He and his tiny wife were from Peking. They must have had at least ten children and dozens of relatives. The Chinese, I have been told, are taught at an early age to speak loud and clearly; indeed, all day long I heard many loud voices drifting from their home. When the whole clan gathered for an evening meal or a celebration, I heard the obvious sounds from early morning presaging the event: the chop, chop, chopping of vegetables and meats. Then in the afternoon I smelled the fragrance of Mandarin cooking wafting toward our house.

When it was harvest time for the landlord's ripe mangoes and lichees, of which there was an abundance each year, several members of the boisterous clan climbed up the laden trees to pick the bounty. All during the time of harvesting I was aware of the strange, excited, cacophonous, staccato language of the Chinese.

More hands were needed to accomplish the variety of jobs in the factory; my father hired a carpenter, a painter, and a general helper-janitor. The latter, named Nam Koong, was a short, wiry man with sparse greying hair and a moon-faced grin. He was the constant butt of ridicule. Besides, he had a yellowed cockeye and a good-natured vulnerability. Although everybody liked him, he was ordered around with shouts and taunts. "Nam Koong, you fool, come here! Sweep up this mess!" He would respond by running with a broom. Another would cry, "Koong, you so-and-so, go out with the driver." He would drop whatever he was doing and obey the command.

The aged Ordway was a trial to my mother. Whenever he encountered her Ordway reared his frame up straight, as if to prepare for combat. He and Mother always seemed to be at odds. She watched him out of the corner of her eye as he took time out several times a day to roll a cigarette and puff away. He never threw tacks into his mouth; his constant cough prevented that. He picked up tacks one by one from a box and pressed each into the piece of furniture he was working on. Mother was not only annoyed with his work habits but also because he lived rent-free in a room above the store. She suggested Ordway pay rent for his lodging, but Father would not hear of it. He remembered too well how Ordway had taught him to write invoices, to address a prospective customer, and to prepare a job description. Many a night Father made use of what he learned from Ordway: poring over books and making entries in his scratchy, illegible handwriting.

We children lived in the midst of dust. My brothers and I had nowhere to play but in and near the cemented area between the store and the carpenter shop. Inevitably we developed allergies that remained with us for life. We breathed in the powdery shavings of the wood saw. We inhaled the exhaust from the hand-grinding machine, which spewed puffed-up cotton and resilient black hair used for stuffing furniture. The upholsterers were in the habit of patting or slapping the seat and back of the furniture they were working on to give it a smooth, rounded look. Clouds of dust swirled about continually, settling in our hair and clogging our noses and lungs. Much of the dust rose and settled upstairs in our apartment. When my father's business was very good, we were literally bathed in dust.

Our neighbors had reasons to complain—the terribly noisy machinery in the factory, the annoying dust, and the paint fumes. But they never did. They were probably too engrossed in their struggle of making a go of their own businesses. The Japanese merchants included a tailor, a dressmaker, and a barber on one side of us. On the other side were a Chinese druggist and a Portuguese hardware man.

I believed that if it weren't for Mother, my father would never have become a success. She had little patience with his propensity to go off in a corner and indulge in "trying out something" with his hands whenever business happened to be going well. She made up with practical common sense what she may have lacked in imagination and humor. Her approach was "cut and save whenever possible," whereas my father's was "stop often and tell stories"—whether it was about covering a Queen Anne chair or about repairing a tool. He laughed often and enjoyed his own stories. If Mother happened to be near him at such times, she advised, "Cut out the talk and get on with the job."

Although it was the Depression era, there were many wealthy people living in fine homes in Hawaii who required the services of my father from time to time. He not only reupholstered their period furniture but also made built-to-order accessories and tropical pieces for their lanais.

The oversized, custom-made couch called the *hikie* became a specialty at King Furniture Co. It was a very large, deeply comfortable, luxurious piece of furniture for sitting or lying down. The springs in it were hand tied, over which were laid layers of cotton and hair, then it was upholstered with a sturdy, expensive fabric that could withstand long wear. Banked on the sides and the back of the *hikie* were throw pillows in bright colors.

Some of the larger *hikie* took as many as fifty to seventy pillows.

For many years I thought my father's business was like a terrible monster whose maw was always open wide, demanding endless feeding of money. But when business was good I was relaxed and at peace. My father was proud that his half-ton truck was paid for at last and he could invest in a new and faster sewing machine.

Just when everything seemed to be going well, there erupted a sudden war of words between my parents over money. Father said, "No, no, we can't afford to move to a house away from here."

Mother retorted, "Yes, we can. And it's about time we got out of this prison we call home. We can't even hear a visitor knocking on our front door—our front door is the front door of the store! We need a parlor so that our daughter can receive gentlemen callers."

CHAPTER 9

Taking a Gamble

THE whine of the bandsaw, fretful sputter of the cotton grinder, and endless roar of the sewing machine I preferred to the constant quarrels between my parents as to whether it was a good time for our family to move from the factory. I prayed for a quick resolution to the problem.

To my relief my prayer was answered. One day there ensued a peace. It seemed Father had won over the arguments raised by Mother when he expressed a genuine fear and lack of confidence that he would be able to meet the rents for both the factory and a home. Mother was subdued. No mention was made again of the factory being an unsuitable home for us. But I knew she had not given up. Her desire to live in a nice neighborhood of houses with trees and flowers was too strong.

The hard times seemed to be over; the business was flourishing. In the factory my mother steadily provided the three upholsterers with stitched pieces of fabric for covering chairs and couches. Anyone who watched the four of them would have noticed the rhythm of their jobs, as if they were following a master conductor; none fell out of step or time—except Ordway occasionally when he stopped to roll a cigarette or succumb to a cough.

Then one day after school as I walked in the store I heard what sounded like a renewal of the verbal battles between my parents.

"Oh, shut up! Leave me alone," Father shouted.

I felt embarrassed. The employees became unusually quiet. The janitor, Nam Koong, glancing around sheepishly, tried to keep his usual grin suppressed. Ordway held his cough. After the workers went home, instead of coming up to the apartment to start dinner, Mother went into the carpenter shop and confronted Father.

"Yobo, we could have sent out the Schaeffer order today if you had helped," she began. "What were you doing?"

"I was busy," he muttered, without looking up.

"Busy with what? What're you doing?"

"I think—pretty soon—I'll have a new invention ready."

"Wh-a-a-t!" Mother cried. "How can you waste time like that? Don't you see we have so much work to do?"

He was so absorbed in the bamboo material in his hand he was not paying attention.

In disgust she swore, *"Ji-rral! ji-rral!"* and left him.

My mother began taking unannounced trips to town during the day. The trips grew more and more frequent, often bringing her home just in time for her to make dinner. She always took my baby sister with her. Father was annoyed; the upholsterers stood idle unless *he* sat down and did the sewing himself.

"Where have you been all day?" he asked Mother late one afternoon.

"I had some business to do."

"What kind of business?"

"Oh, this and that. And I visited my friend, Pil Soon."

Father looked incredulous. "You mean you went *holo holo* on a work day? When there's so much to do in the shop?"

"You have lots of workers now," she retorted. She took a package of meat from the ice chest and unwrapped the pink butcher paper. "You don't need me now."

"But the sewing is piling up!"

Mother said nothing. She sliced the pork in thin strips, then opened the ice chest again and pulled out a head of cabbage.

"Damn! damn!" Father stalked out of the kitchen.

After a moment his agitation cooled, and he shuffled back to the kitchen. "Will you help tomorrow?" he begged. "We must ship the Baldwin order to Maui. They're having a big party this weekend. We must get the furniture on the next freighter."

"All right," Mother agreed to help.

The next day my father and mother and everyone in the factory worked at top speed on the Baldwin job. We never could tell whether a customer was speaking the truth about a party schedule or whether it was just a ruse to get our staff to deliver an order fast. But it always worked. Sometimes it meant the employees had to work longer hours or go without lunch or make some other sacrifice.

Things went smoothly for a long while at work and at home. Then one evening a casual remark by Mother ignited a small explosion. She said, "I think it's about time we lived like other people—in a house."

Father replied curtly, "Don't bring that up again. You know we can't afford to." He was reading the *Nippu Jiji*. He usually put in extra hours in the shop after dinner, but he must have felt tired that night.

"Why not?" Mother raised her voice. "We've paid all the big debts, haven't we? We own the truck now. We got a nice new power sewing machine."

"No. Still too many expenses to worry about."

"We can manage, I'm sure," Mother insisted.

"No!" came the reply. "I said *no!* I don't want to hear about this anymore." He folded the paper noisily, stood up, and went to bed.

I knew my mother would not give up. This time she didn't look vulnerable or defeated as she had a few months before.

After getting us ready for school in the morning, she took the baby in a basket and went down to work in the shop. She worked many hours each day.

Leaving Father at home fussing with his new invention idea, the rest of our family walked the mile or so to church each Sunday. Mother did not bother him. She said, "He has to play with his new toy. Let him."

In the summer on lazy Sunday afternoons when there were no church meetings, or in the evenings when the apartment became unbearably hot and humid, we went riding in my father's truck.

We piled into the truck, the baby and our parents in the front and my brothers and I in the open truck bed. One day we cruised leisurely along the quiet streets of Honolulu, on Beretania and King, on to Kalakaua, to Diamond Head, then to Kapiolani and up to Wilder. We enjoyed the cool, fresh air. Soon we found ourselves driving through an area thick with trees, tangled vines, and wild brush. We stopped. It was then I heard an angry exchange of words between my mother and father. Suddenly the truck jerked to a start and speeded out of the wooded area. My brothers and I clung to each other to keep from being tossed about. When we finally came to a halt in front of our store, Father jumped out and strode to the small side entry. He unlocked the door and vanished inside.

I was breathless and nervous. "Omoni, what was that about? What's the matter with Abuji?"

"Oh, I don't know what's wrong with your father. He gets mad every time I talk about getting a nice house for us."

I realized this was the pattern of the way things went. Time after time what Mother wanted, Father opposed at first. She'd bring it up again, he'd bellow and resist, until, somehow, his opposition and resistance were gradually chipped away and he acquiesced to her wishes.

She tried not to provoke him in any way. She left him alone to dwell in his dream world of fancy ideas. He could come and go as he pleased, slipping into fantasy and returning to the work in the factory.

I believe it finally came to the point when Father was willing to let Mother have her wish to have the family move to a rented cottage where there would be flowers, trees, and a green lawn. But Mother asked for something more. She announced she was interested in building a house in a new subdivision.

"Do you know what that will cost?" he asked.

"Yes. About five thousand dollars."

Father's face contorted with disbelief. "Five thousand dollars?"

"Yes."

He broke into a laugh. "I thought I didn't hear right the first time you said it. Huh, you know we can't afford that."

"Why not?" was Mother's quick rejoinder.

"Do you know what those builders want as a down payment?"

"Yes." Mother seemed to have all the answers to questions Father might have. "One thousand dollars."

"One thousand dollars? And where in hell do you expect me to get that kind of money? Impossible! No one will lend me that much." He dismissed the whole idea with a sweep of his hand.

Two months later my father opened the front door of the store and admitted a number of friends from the Korean community. It was early evening. He led them up to our apartment. I noticed they all looked very businesslike, so this was obviously not a social call. Mother joined them in the living room with pencils and small squares of paper.

She spoke warmly, thanking the guests for coming. She extended an invitation to them to return the first day of each month thereafter to take part in the *kye*.

Three men and five women guests were present. Each handed fifty dollars to Mother. From a small cloth bag with a drawstring closure Mother drew out more currency. She counted: five hundred fifty dollars from the cloth bag and four hundred from the guests. Then Mother went into the bedroom and brought fifty dollars to add as her share to the pot.

She announced, "I have one thousand dollars here. Let us begin bidding." Mother passed out the squares of paper and the pencils. She took one square and a pencil herself.

This was the first meeting of the *kye* that my father and mother organized. *Kye* was the Korean immigrant's way of obtaining a loan from a group of very reliable friends. No official documents were drawn. The honor of the parties involved was the basis of trust.

Since it was my parents who wished to borrow one thousand dollars for the down payment on a house, they initiated the organization of this group. Twenty people willing to put up fifty dollars per month for twenty consecutive months were asked to participate.

It was understood that the initiator of the *kye* would "win the pot" the first month; bidding by the eight participants present that evening was just a ritual. Mother jotted two dollars on her square of paper. The other bids that evening were presumably much lower. After announcing her bid as the highest, Mother gave out two dollars to each of the guests and put aside twenty-four dollars for those participants who were not present. The highest bid was deemed the interest earned for the month by each investor in the *kye*.

The following month any one of the other nineteen participants could vie for the pot. If no one urgently needed cash, the bids would be low. However, since risk was always a factor, strong competitive bidding usually took place. Often it was a game of wits as to who could pay out the smallest amount, or interest, for the one thousand dollar pot. *Kye* proceedings were closely monitored by those involved in their investment.

Thus my parents secured the thousand-dollar loan at about 2 percent interest. They immediately negotiated with the real estate broker to build a house for us at the foot of Makiki Round Top, a subdivision that looked like a forest at the time, with new roads and utility lines installed.

For the remainder of the *kye* term of nineteen months, my parents were bound to contribute fifty dollars per month to the pot, expect no other income from the fund, and operate the *kye* for the benefit of the other participants.

Five months after the precious one thousand dollars was given to the real estate agency, our new home at the foot of Makiki Round Top on Nehoa Street was completed. The three-bedroom, one-bath house, painted white, stood in the middle of tall weeds. A sidewalk from the street led to the red cement steps and the porch. A three-tiered, flat-top arrangement of red cement rose alongside the steps in place of a bannister. These flat tops were ideal places for showing off potted plants.

Ours was the only house on Nehoa Street. Across the street was a jungle of shrubs, grasses, and trees, with vines weaving between their branches. My brothers exclaimed, "Heh, we can play over there. We'll have fun climbing the trees!"

What none of us had expected was the utter solitude of the place. There were perhaps two or three houses about a mile away. The days were quiet; the nights spooky. I don't think we noticed or appreciated the clean air. After having spent years growing up in a factory, we children had to get used to the awful hush that greeted us each morning and persisted through the day.

We tried to be enthusiastic about our new house. We said it was nice to walk on solid floors with no hint of termites. There was a pleasant, uncrowded feeling about the place. The bedrooms were compact, but the living-dining area was huge. The dining set, a rectangular table with six chairs, looked lost, as if floating in a sea of space. The many windows in the room left little or no wall space for pictures.

Mother found herself drawn more and more to the yard. Weeds were growing rampant in the virgin soil. She knew no one would tackle them if she didn't herself. She comforted herself with the thought that at least the lot was no bigger than seventy-five hundred square feet.

My brothers and I walked to our schools. Mother stayed home with our baby sister and they spent most of the day outside. Soon both of their faces were baked brown. To Mother, clearing the weeds appeared to be an endless task.

We wondered how long it would be before more people moved into the subdivision. One day we passed a house under construction about five blocks away from ours. Mother stopped to ask one of the carpenters why they were so slow in putting up houses in the area.

The Japanese workman scratched his head. "Nobody wanna buy. People scared!" Putting down his hammer, the man lit a cigarette. "Now is hard times. They think it's gonna get worse."

"Why?" Mother asked.

"Bad all over, Missus. Mainland, too. Nobody got money. People scared this Depression. You know, some of these houses already sold—then owners back out. They think this Depression gonna wipe them out. They don't wanna take chance."

The year was 1931. When my mother heard that the Depression and hard times were plaguing the island she must have been surprised. For many years she had believed it was only the immigrants from the old countries who were poor and had to struggle to gain a foothold in the economy. She had thought all others, especially the Americans, were rich.

The years following 1931, the year of the house purchase, were bad. Father worried because his customers were less and less inclined to refurbish their furniture. So often he was saying, "The employees don't have enough to do." The mortgage payments and the *kye* dues weighed heavily on his head. He blamed Mother and our new house again and again for his financial woes.

And Mother was stricken with terrible misgivings; perhaps she had been too hasty in taking the gamble of investing in a piece of property. She was speaking loud enough for me to hear one day, although I'm sure she was talking to herself, "I regret the day I told your father 'I've found just the place I want to live'."

In the meantime she was annoyed to see my father "fooling around" with a new invention idea. She was sure he was wasting time and money. If only he showed more sense, she thought, life would not be so hard for them. The last patent he had secured on the chimney plate had brought him some success— enough money to start his own business. He had been forced to sell the last chimney plates to a small hardware merchant because he could not find the time to manufacture any more.

After school each day my brothers and I walked over to the shop and waited there for the ride home with our parents when the store closed. It seemed we spent more hours in the factory than in our home in Makiki.

CHAPTER 10

A Successful Invention at Last

DURING the Depression, instead of laying off his employees, my father engaged them in testing his newest patent idea. He brightened the large showroom by adding more lightbulbs. The plain walls of the store were covered with displays of his innovative bamboo blinds and draperies. The upholsterers Yin Hong and Jimmie learned to install the bamboo hangings under cornices, which were built and painted by the carpenter and the painter. Only old Ordway hammered and coughed in the background, working on the few reupholstery jobs that trickled in.

My mother looked with anxiety on these efforts to keep the employees busy. She must have thought they were all crazy spending day after day playing with Father's toys.

To her amazement, his invention began to sell. One wealthy client after another replaced their worn, faded draperies with new draperies made of bamboo. Furthermore, the new bamboo installed in their homes promoted sales of rattan-trimmed custom furniture. The clients enjoyed the tropical setting created in their homes by combining bamboo draperies and rattan furniture.

The bamboo material, which came from Japan, was made up of one-sixteenth inch split bamboo strips woven together with heavy threads. The green peel, or bark, of the bamboo pole from which the drapery material was made was extremely durable.

In Honolulu the best-known importer of Japanese goods was the firm Iida. My father bought dozens of ready-made blinds from Iida, then stripped and discarded the pulleys and cords attached to them; the horizontal strips of bamboo in Iida's roll-up shade then could be turned to work in vertical strips in a drapery. It wasn't long before he realized how foolish he was to squander money and labor purchasing the shades and dismantling them before converting the bamboo material into draw draperies.

As sales of the new draperies increased, a way was found to import the bamboo material in continuous rolls, like cloth yardage. The shipments of woven, peel, split bamboo began arriving in rolls of one hundred running feet. They were warehoused above the store. The rolls looked strange, standing like thick stumps of trees of varying heights lined up for inspection. A few rolls came in three foot heights; most were five, six, and seven feet tall—the heights needed most frequently for windows and doors in Hawaii's homes. Later, rolls of eight, nine, and ten feet were ordered for the arches and windows in commercial buildings.

The new bamboo came raw and unfinished, unlike the polished staves of the blinds from Iida. So the material had to be blow-torched to remove loose, needly fibers. Yin Hong or Jimmie lay a cut-to-measure piece of the material over two horses and swung the blow torch back and forth until the surface was smooth enough for one's hand to run over it without feeling splinters.

My father was the best salesman for the new bamboo draw draperies and the new bamboo folding shade—his two innovations for windows. He could speak for hours extolling their virtues with irresistible enthusiasm. A skillful craftsman and an adept handyman, he promised he could make his inventions fit any window, no matter how different it was from the ordinary. And he promised the bamboo would last the customer's lifetime, although he had no proof. He believed it was important to hem the sharp edges of the cut bamboo with a cotton tape, which my mother sewed on. Our super-power sewing machine ran easily over the woody fibers. Soon Yin Hong and Jimmie became installers of these draperies and blinds in homes all over the city.

I wondered how my father was able to handle draperies with

such proficiency. Then I recalled the experience he had while at Bailey Furniture Co., especially one time when he was involved with the "fanciest curtains" he had ever seen. The Princess Theatre on Fort Street, which in Honolulu in the 1920s served as a first-class movie theatre and symphony hall, had called on my father to take charge of the replacement of the proscenium curtains. For several nights he sat next to me at the kitchen table in the Pele Street house while I studied, making crude drawings of swirling drapes on wrapping paper. He arranged and rearranged the pattern of loose, flowing folds: a sheer inner curtain that parted gracefully to the sides and the heavy upper curtains rising to reveal the full stage. He hummed as he worked with numbers—how many yards of soft material? How many folds per swirl? How many swirls in all? I asked at one point what the heavy marks on the side in one drawing represented. He replied, "Those are the ties, the tassels."

There came a time when my father felt so pressured he said he wished he had twelve pairs of hands. Every custom order of furniture and drapery seemed to require his personal attention. Women cried and begged him for special treatment of their jobs. My poor father was sought after from the moment he opened the doors of the store in the morning. The customers clamored, "Mr. Kwon, *will* you do this for me?" "Mr. Kwon, *can* you do that for me?" Then terse, stronger demands followed: "Kwon, you *must* do this for me!"

He made excuses and offered apologies for late deliveries. He had to resort to telling lies. The sheer diversity of orders required a variety of abilities; an employee often felt stymied and needed help before he could proceed with his work.

My father happened to be on the phone one day talking to an irate woman. He said, "I'm sorry, I hurt my hand—got it caught in a machine." The same woman, looking very sympathetic, inquired a week later when she stopped in the store, "How is your hand?" He asked, "What hand?" When the woman reminded him of her call, he hastily replied, "Oh, that—it's all okay now."

When he ran out of excuses, apologies, and lies he decided to hide himself far back in the carpenter shop where no one could find him.

There was one woman, however, who was clever enough to ferret him out of hiding. Not believing that "Mr. Kwon is not here," she brushed aside all the employees who tried to stop her from entering the carpenter shop. Dressed in shorts and zori slippers, wearing huge sunglasses, Doris Duke Cromwell, the tobacco heiress, swept through the shop looking for my father. Obviously tired of peddlers of goods fawning over her, she found my father refreshing and a challenge. But he did not favor her. In fact, he did not particularly care to do business with her. He said she was overly demanding and demeaning. She haggled over the price of every item. Perhaps because she had years of fending off cheaters, she had acquired a style of bartering when buying.

He found her especially unreasonable with *time*. He did not mind if she acted like many other women who expected special attention. But when he was forced to make an appointment at 5:30 P.M. at her home, a most inconvenient hour for a man who started work at 5:30 A.M., and he was made to wait and wait once he got to her home until her swim lesson with Duke Kahanamoku was over, he was angry. Her maid, feeling sorry for him, offered to take him on a tour of the tobacco heiress' home, the famous Shangri-la at Black Point, which was just being completed. But he told her he was too tired.

But my father had great respect for most of his clients, especially the gracious *kamaaina* wives of wealthy businessmen in Hawaii. He referred to them as "ladies." He noted their modulated voices, their expressions of appreciation, their trust in his billing as fair.

My mother, who had to divide her time between the shop and home, found little time to rest. She even had to give up regular church attendance. Our house on Nehoa Street, she said, needed so much of her attention. She alone had planted all the grass around the house, a coconut tree in the front, and an avocado tree in the back. A lawnmower was purchased and we depended on Father to push it occasionally around the property. After six days at the factory, my mother spent most of her Sunday cleaning the house and washing clothes. Every Sunday I helped with the laundry—most of which was boiled in soapy water in a five-gallon square tin, set up outside over a crude arrangement of stones. I didn't understand why we had to go through the arduous task of stirring, boiling, and retrieving the laundry, carrying it dripping to the wash trays in the garage to be rinsed. We hoped for sunny Sundays, for the wash could be dried on the lines outside, then ironed in the afternoon. On Sunday nights we could sleep on crisp, clean, pressed sheets and our clothes for the week would be ready.

We all felt an urgent need to save time somehow. My father had the idea that if he bought a family car, then Mother would not have to take the bus to the shop. She could then spend more time at the store.

The difficult task of teaching her to drive the new Ford Model A touring car fell on him. What stormy driving lessons they must have had, for when they returned from one he would be shouting as they walked in the house: "I told you to step on the brake *and* clutch at the same time. Why do you forget? How many times must I remind you?"

She looked indignant but determined to succeed. We children cheered her, and made faces at her instructor when he wasn't looking. We couldn't wait for her to get her license and take us riding in the open green car with the narrow running board.

One day when we got home we noticed part of the jungle across from our house was being cleared. We were pleased; we could be expecting neighbors soon. As we had hoped, one house started going up, then another. Then we found both houses torn down several weeks later and the ground leveled. What was going on?

Trees and shrubs were being cut down every day until the area looked cleared for about twenty or more houses. The bald ground revealed a gently rising slope from Nehoa Street. The land rose sharply and met the hill behind; steep ridges and bare clefts showed.

Instead of houses, one large building began to take shape. Its architecture was Mediterranean; its roofing, colorful tile. Before it was completed we learned it was to be the new Roosevelt High School. The new building when finished looked stark—like a fortress or a prison—situated alone on a rise of the land. But later, with plantings around the structure, the lines of the school softened. Roosevelt graduated its first class of seniors at the location in June 1933, and I was one of them.

At the beginning of that summer my mother started packing for a trip to Korea. I had been so excited about graduation and planning for college I hadn't been aware of my mother's plans.

"Omoni, where are you going?" I asked.

"Oh, don't you know, Chung Sook? I'm going to visit my—my—parents." Her eyes misted and she made an effort to control her tears by biting her lips.

"Why? Are they ill?" My grandparents' son, a doctor, would be able to care for them. "Are they very ill?"

"No. I don't think so. But there is something not quite right going on there. I have to go and see . . ."

"This trip is sudden, isn't it?" I said to her. "How long will you be gone? Just for the summer?"

"I cannot say. I hope I can come back soon."

The words sounded ominous. A lump formed in my throat. I was more concerned, I was ashamed to admit, about myself faring at home without Mother than for her safety. "It's going to be hard for us without you, Omoni. Maybe I should stay out of college this year if you plan to stay a while."

"No. No. You will be able to manage, I'm sure. Your father says you can look for someone to come in and help with the housework and the cooking while I'm gone. Remember this: your father and I insist you register to enter the University of Hawaii this fall. You must get an education. No matter what happens at home."

CHAPTER 11

Greed and Inhumanity

I HAD not anticipated that taking over as cook and housekeeper would be so hard. I missed my mother. My brothers were recalcitrant. They refused to accept me as surrogate mother, so we continually quarreled over who should do the chores.

Fortunately I soon found help. Doris, a student from McKinley High School, responded to a "help wanted" request to the school counselor. She came everyday after school to do light house cleaning, washing, and assisting me with dinner. She ate with us, then cleaned up the dinner dishes before going home.

How tedious it was to plan the daily menu. Whenever possible, I rushed home from the university where I was a freshman to catch the Japanese grocery vendor, who traveled in the Makiki, McCully, and Manoa neighborhoods. His Ford wagon looked as if it traveled on four flat tires, so loaded was it with meats, produce, canned goods, and pickled foods. He used a trembling scale with a round face to weigh slices of beef, pork, or fish. The vegetables stayed surprisingly fresh, even on the hottest days. He sold a bunch of watercress for a nickel; also priced at five cents was a block of tofu, a handful of scallions, or a bag of dried shrimp. He carried bread and sausage for breakfast, too.

In November that year a flu epidemic hit Honolulu. My brothers and I were victims, and we lay in bed with body aches and high fevers. We crawled to the bathroom. We could not eat, for if we did we only threw up. Sick as we were for over three weeks, we never thought of calling a doctor because we thought we had just a cold. Doris stayed away. Amazingly, through all the weeks we children were laid up, Father escaped the flu.

Christmas and New Year, the festive holidays for families, were lonely without Mother. If she were at home, we would have had the house full of friends dropping in and celebrating with us. No one remembered us except Ajumani, the lady who cared for our sister while Mother was away. We were invited to her house for the traditional *dduk kuk* on New Year's Eve, the meal before midnight. How delicious the broth tasted with the rich ingredients floating in it, especially the *dduk*—sticky white slices of pounded-and-cooked rice. The stock was flavored with thin strips of beef marinated in soyu and garnished with egg and dried seaweed. We saw the holiday sweetcakes, which took days to prepare, placed on platters all around Ajumani's dining room and living room.

When word came in late January that my mother was returning home, I looked in the mirror. I hoped she would notice and appreciate how much I'd aged while she was away.

We went down to the pier to greet Mother. What a happy sight to see her coming down the gangplank of the *Taiyo Maru!* She looked well in a blue silk dress with white polka dots, her cheeks pink like those of other Korean women returning from a visit to Korea.

The food my mother brought back was wonderful. The winter kim chee packed in large, heavy, crockery pots tasted like no kim chee made in Honolulu. The flavor was deep, deep, and lingered in the mouth. We bit into chunks of turnip coated with red chili pepper, pink with age. The red and pink cabbage had such an incredible taste that we did not want to stop eating it. And the dried pickled fish, dark and exotic in appearance, was strangely tangy and peppery at the same time. My brothers, however, could not stand the strong aroma of these foods. Whenever one of the crockery pots was opened, they cried, "Ooh, stink! stink! We don't want to eat that!" and ran out of the kitchen.

On that first evening of my mother's return we sat around the kitchen table and talked. I asked, "How are Grandma and Grandpa?"

Mother nodded her head reflectively as she spoke, "I believe they are all right. You know, Chung Sook, compared to the time you and I were there, things are very different now in Taegu."

"Oh? In what way?"

"The first thing I noticed when I reached my parents' home was—your uncle's medical building was shut down."

"Why? What happened to him? Isn't he practicing anymore?"

Mother spoke very slowly, "We don't know where he is. Or what he's doing or whether he's alive."

I couldn't believe what I was hearing. "What—?"

"We don't know. We do hope he's alive. If he is, then he's probably in Manchuria with other men who ran away from Korea."

"Manchuria!" I exclaimed. I had heard somewhere—was it in one of my classes?—that Manchuria was a hotbed for communists. Had my uncle turned communist? The word struck terror in me. Was my uncle a political fanatic? How could he have left his parents and run off?

In the days that followed I was able to put together bits and pieces of more information on the conditions in Korea and the plight of the people. My father always listened to these reports with grave concern. At first I thought my grandparents were in bad financial trouble because their son had abandoned them. But I gradually understood this was not so.

After the March 1, 1919, revolution, according to Mother, the Japanese government had been determined to stamp out more outbreaks of rebellion. Japan altered its militaristic control of Korea to what the Koreans recognized as a cultural control. Koreans became imperial subjects of the emperor of Japan. In schools, students could converse only in Japanese. On the streets and in the marketplace, only Japanese was spoken. In the area of spiritual reform, Koreans were forced to give up their Christian beliefs and their churches, forced to visit the Japanese ancestral shrines, and to bow in the direction of the emperor's palace at a certain hour each day.

Most painful and degrading of the changes was economic. No Korean could amass wealth. Many members of the *yangban* class, who had owned large tracts of land for centuries, began losing their holdings because their farmers could not meet the increasing government quotas to grow enough rice to feed the Japanese.

A world-wide food crisis had begun at the end of World War I. In Japan the rice shortage had been so acute that numerous rice riots had occurred.

The Japanese government found it convenient to make Koreans their victims of the rice shortage. To increase rice production Japan formed a plan in 1920; this plan was still being enforced in Korea while my mother was visiting in 1933 and 1934.

Korea was made almost solely a one-crop country—to raise enough rice to feed the Japanese. Year after year the demands had increased and many Korean farmers found it impossible to satisfy the imperialists in command. Most Koreans, except the wealthiest landowners, ate little or no white rice; they had to buy an inferior type of cheap grain from Manchuria—millet—which was in short supply and which they hated. While the Japanese were fed and fattened, thousands of Koreans were dying each year from hunger.

Although my grandfather had lost a considerable amount of his land, fortunately he still retained enough workers and land to meet production expectations.

My mother explained with bitterness, "The Japanese commander came to your uncle to force him to close his clinic and work on his land so that he could push his farmers to greater production. Most of the well-to-do merchants and professionals were ordered to give up their shops and practices."

Smoothing her brow as if to ease the pain, my mother concluded, "Your uncle could not tolerate the idea of giving up his clinic to raise rice. So he ran away and probably hid for months. We think he eventually escaped to Manchuria. We know there's a big anti-Japanese movement growing there. We hope he managed to escape . . ."

After her return from Korea, the first day she drove down to the factory, she commented that the store looked shabbier than she remembered. Although she noted handsome new furniture and refurbished overstuffed pieces in one section of the showroom, the main line of business obviously was the bamboo draperies. Yin Hong, Jimmie, and Ordway were taking turns at the power sewing machine; each one depended on himself for his sewing needs. When they saw my mother, they welcomed her with great joy and sighs of relief.

"Mrs. Kwon, how glad we are to see you back! You will sew for us again, won't you?"

"I see you are managing well without me," she replied with a commending smile.

"No, no. See how *kapakahi* our sewing is." They pointed to the crude, sometimes awry, stitching on bamboo and on fabrics.

So my mother was back at her power sewing job. It wasn't long before she experienced the familiar, overwhelming stresses of trying to accomplish the myriad of tasks at home and at the shop. She remarked one day, "I don't know why but I feel like I'm in some kind of race all the time." Because she was bent forward over the machine almost all day long, she used to say she wished someone would reverse her chest and back so she could straighten her body with ease.

Some weeks later on a Saturday morning when I dropped in at the store, I came upon my parents engaged in intense conversation. My mother looked calm but my father was obviously agitated.

"Damn, why does the landlord have to raise the rent? That Chinaman. He thinks I'm making a fortune."

He paced back and forth, baring his teeth as he usually did when he was angry. He said, "This rotten old building—why, it's ready to fall down. So termite eaten. That Chinaman, he's money mad, that's all."

Then he stood still and was very quiet. He leaned against the worktable, deep in thought. Slowly he declared, "I know what we'll do. We'll move! That's it. I'll find another place—another shop. Why should we stay here?"

In a few months my father found another location for his business. But it was not a vacant store or an empty building. It was a piece of property on Beretania Street, half a block away from the present shop. On the property were four rental cottages. Father said he could conduct his business in two of the houses and leave the other two rented. Since the property contained ten thousand square feet, he envisioned several structures on it eventually: an office building, a factory, and a warehouse.

My mother, the practical one, questioned the feasibility of his plan. "You mean you're going to squeeze all your employees and all the stock and all the machinery into the two small family dwellings?" She shook her head in dismay.

"We're not staying here any longer than we have to," he replied. "I'm not fattening the landlord's purse any more. Let him try to find a tenant for this rotten place."

My parents again organized a *kye* among their most trusted friends to secure the down payment for the purchase of the new property.

Everyday as we drove home we passed the future site of the business. There were four small, unimposing family dwellings set back from the street, with unkempt grass around them. Except for the Honolulu Rapid Transit carbarn on the corner of Alapai and Beretania, the whole block was made up of scattered groupings of two- and three-bedroom cottages.

Moving day came. As my mother had feared and predicted, an accumulation of tools, machinery, paints, rolls of fabric and bamboo, and countless other items came out of nowhere to be moved. The company pick-up truck probably made a hundred trips to transport everything to the houses. The houses bulged with all the goods the employees piled into them in no particular order.

At the end of the day, surveying the crowded cottages, my mother uttered, "This is pure chaos. This is the devil's work."

She knew the other two houses on the lot could not be vacated of the tenants because the rent from them was needed to help meet the mortgage payments. She sighed, addressing my father,

"Yobo, you are a most impractical man. I don't know how you expect to carry on business here."

It took the employees over a month to get oriented to the new quarters. They were continually elbowing or running into each other. They kept misplacing their tools, then sometimes spent hours looking for them.

In the front cottage the desk phone occupied a space next to the sewing machine. More than half of the incoming calls were probably drowned by the roar of the machine. And when someone did use the phone, the machine had to stop.

Before long my father realized the telephone, the lifeline of the business, had to be placed away from the factory. He hired a contractor to draw plans for a small, new concrete building to serve as the office and showroom.

When completed the structure looked beautiful and modern, with two picture windows, double glass doors between them, a side window overlooking the carbarn, and a solid metal door on the opposite side to the driveway. A two-and-a-half-inch thick metal sliding door provided a fireproof partition between the office and the first cottage.

A new sign with a new name was hung from the roof awning in front of the shop. My father decided to call his business D. Kwon & Co. About that time Mr. Ordway felt he should retire. We were sad to see him go, but glad for him.

I was terribly upset the day I heard our family had to move again—this time to one of the rental cottages next to the factory. Back to the dust, the fumes, the noise! I wept for days. We would be sliding down the scale of decent living.

My mother tried to comfort me. "Can't you understand why we must move out of this house on Nehoa? You know this is a very nice house in a beautiful neighborhood. Your father knows he can get more rent from this house than any down there next to the factory. He needs cash desperately now."

"But I hear he's thinking of putting up more buildings. Then where is he going to get the money for that?" I countered.

"Well, he would want to be close to the construction site. That's the only reason I can think of. We'll be returning to the Nehoa house just as soon as we can."

So our family moved again. The shabby house we went into was surprisingly large, with three bedrooms, a kitchen, a good-sized living room, and a front and back porch, both enclosed. But the sounds of the machines and the smells of paints were inescapable.

CHAPTER 12

The Miyoshi Bamboo

To survive as a businessman in Hawaii it was necessary for my father to speak better English than the average immigrant launderer or tailor or grocer, for his business catered to the wealthy and the educated. He listened intently to the cadences in their speech and tried to imitate them when he spoke. The imitation combined with pidgin was nothing resembling classroom English. There was a certain affectation and swagger in his manner of speaking. Nonetheless he must have sounded sincere and knowledgeable, for he was adored by his women customers and respected by the men. He learned to spell certain nouns and verbs for trade purposes so that he could bill his customers; for example, "Recover 1 Arm Chair," "Install 2 pr. Curtains in Living Room," "Repair 1 Queen Anne Chair Leg."

He did not have the capital to invest in ready-made furniture to sell, so he had to offer a wide variety of services. Labor was cheap compared to the cost of goods; a shopowner without capital was forced to work long hours with his hands. To lure customers away from other furniture dealers in the city, my father used ingenious ideas in repairing, remodeling, and refurbishing chairs, sofas, tables, draperies, and blinds. Not only did he tighten sagging springs and plump lifeless cushions, but he saved a broken yet treasured heirloom or even made a reasonable copy of it. He built inexpensive but elegant-looking square tables without the oldfashioned curves, ornate carvings, and rounded legs that were part of most traditional furniture. When other upholsterers said it could not be done, he stretched a limited quantity of a customer's expensive yardage to recover a wing chair or a Louis XIV sofa. Once a woman pleaded, "Mr.

Kwon, I wish you could hang a wood blind outside for me to shade my room on the second floor so that I can operate the blind from inside the house." He did just that to her great satisfaction.

The specialty shopowners who desired unique showrooms called on my father for help. Tina Leser, who was a well-known dress designer as well as owner of a resort shop in Waikiki, had clients from all over the world. They raved over the unusual settings against which her gowns and leisure wear were displayed. They delighted in the touches of rattan poles, bamboo weaves, *koa* and *ohia* woods, and bright fabrics in the decor.

At the end of one job of remodeling her showrooms, Tina Leser remarked she wished she could show her appreciation in some special way. "Kwon, do you and your wife go dancing?" she asked.

He was taken completely by surprise. "What—what you mean?"

"I want to do something nice for you. You've been such a help. But I don't make men's clothes. I could make a nice dress for your wife to wear to a ball."

Still a little confused but guessing what she meant, he broke into a laugh. "Naw, we don't dance."

She then asked, "Do you have a daughter?"

He nodded. "My older daughter is eighteen."

She made a suggestion.

That night when my father told me I could have a ball gown made by one of Hawaii's leading designers, I was filled with pride and intrigue. But I hesitated.

A few weeks later I gathered courage to go by bus all the way to Waikiki to meet the dress designer. As I entered her low, one-story white bungalow on Kalakaua Avenue, I recognized the familiar bamboo draperies gracing the double-hung windows and the dressing rooms. Through the split bamboo drapes I could see the Moana Hotel across the street and tourists alighting from taxis at its entrance. I noticed other tourists promenading the sidewalks on both sides of Kalakaua Avenue, many of them wearing freshly woven, green coconut hats.

Tina Leser, a rather large but well-proportioned woman, surveyed me. She had a preoccupied look, yet her glance was quick. I noticed a flicker of dismay pass over her face. Oh, my, I wondered, what have I done wrong?

She began, "The gown I had in mind for you takes twenty-five yards of organza—white silk organza—with a pattern of multihued fish handpainted by an artist." She walked around me. I was losing my courage. I wished I could disappear through the floor.

I glanced around and saw elegantly dressed customers moving around in the shop. They were all tall and willowy, or tall and stout. Suddenly I realized why Miss Leser was dismayed. My mother usually used only three yards of material to make me a dress. I was five-foot-two and weighed only a hundred pounds. Twenty-five yards would surely overpower me.

Then I heard, "Miss Kwon, I wanted to do something for your father—" She led me to a mannequin standing in a soft, white, billowy dress. "This is my lastest design—a ball gown with a Hawaiian motif. We sell it for a hundred and fifty dollars. I want you to have a dress like this."

I gulped. I never imagined a dress could cost so much. It was lovely. I was mesmerized by the delicate colored fishes swimming around the full skirt in waters that turned from green to pink to purple to blue.

Then I was jolted back to reality by what she said next. "I can make it for you, Miss Kwon, but I'll have to charge you fifty dollars for sewing the dress." What was this—the gift would *cost* me so much? I was speechless.

Miss Leser noticed my discomfort. "You can think it over and let me know if you would like to have this dress."

When I related all that had happened on my visit that afternoon, my father burst out laughing. "She's a smart business-woman!" he chuckled. "Well, tell me, Chung Sook—you want that dress?"

"But fifty dollars—" I protested.

He thought for a moment. I was sure he would agree it was too much. But he said, "If you can find someone to sew it for less, let's get only the material from Miss Leser."

The designer consented to cut all the pieces of the gown with the art work, ready to be sewn together by a dressmaker I had found, who offered to do it for fifteen dollars.

When finished the gown was gorgeous! And it was mine. From the fitted bodice fell layers of swirling white fabric, crisp yet soft and silky, with playful fishes floating in a sea of undulating waves.

I waited several months for an appropriate formal dance. The occasion was the opening of a beautiful ballroom in a new building. I was excited. The huge, smooth dance floor and the open lanais, overlooking the lights of the city to the south and the mountains to the north, looked romantic. Soon I ignored the curious eyes on my gown. Although my date held me a distance from him so as not to crush the fishes on the skirt, still I felt marvelous gliding with him over the polished floor. There were handsome lounge chairs in the lanais, but I stood all night in my high heels.

The construction of the factory was a major operation with many builders working on the project for months. The small, old cottage behind the office building was torn down. Then plain, concrete-block walls reached up to very high ceilings. Long, narrow windows framed in steel were inserted along the walls about twenty feet apart. Each day the structure took on more and more the appearance of a solid, fireproof, capacious factory. When it was completed, my father's employees could not believe the luxury of so much space around them at their work stations. The drapery sewers and traverse track makers were grouped near the front next to the office building, while the painters and the carpenters were quartered toward the back of the immense building.

The employees rarely had a chance to stand idle, for orders were pouring in without pause. No matter how fast they worked they felt they were behind schedule because when customers placed orders they usually wanted them "ready and delivered the next day."

The upholsterers sometimes ran from the factory into the

office to catch the phone ringing. My mother did the best she could to take care of walk-in customers. Everyone in the shop was annoyed because instead of putting his mind to operating the business with optimum efficiency my father busied himself with another pet idea for a patent. The workers shook their heads when they saw him promise a lady his full and prompt attention to her order, then the next moment go off to a corner in the factory—immersed in some creation. He was smitten by the desire to make a venetian blind that would accomplish more functions than the ones on the market.

The public still favored venetian blinds over bamboo draperies for their bedrooms, although they were not totally satisfied with them. Some customers begged, "Mr. Kwon, if you only could make a venetian blind that can drop down from the top so that we can get air through the top. Then we can sleep with our windows and blinds open and get both privacy and air."

My father's newest invention, U.S. Patent No. 2,283,540, made the claim that a venetian blind need not be permanently fixed at the top of the cornice nor fixed at the bottom at the windowsill, and that it could be let down from the top as well as raised from the bottom.

Now that D. Kwon & Co. was manufacturing both bamboo drapes and wood blinds, the twenty-two venetian blind dealers in the city became alarmed. They banded together to discuss how they could prevent Mr. Kwon from ruining them. These nervous men imagined the new patent would drive them all out of business. The alarm spread to California. The wholesale headquarters of venetian blinds on the West Coast sent a representative to Honolulu to study the situation.

The representative stopped by our shop one day unannounced. A large, stern-looking man, wearing spectacles and a tweed suit, asked to see the new type of wood blind being advertised. My father, enjoying nothing better than to show his invention, went into a long, detailed demonstration.

The next day the same man returned, looking sterner than the day before, and asked to see the new type of blind again.

It was not until after an hour of scrutinizing the mechanism

of the blind that he revealed he represented the largest whole-
sale supplier of venetian blinds in the West.

Immediately my father reacted with suspicion and regretted
he had told so much about the patented parts. But what the
man said next stunned him.

"We're willing to give you fifty thousand dollars for your pat-
ent. Then you must stop making this blind." The man empha-
sized the word *stop*. He looked angry and his voice was gruff.

What he offered was so unexpected, so mind-boggling to my
father that he was unable to respond. The man tersely said
before he left, "Think it over and let me know." He left his card
with the name of his hotel.

My parents looked at the offer from all angles. "It's a lot of
money—fifty thousand dollars!" my father repeated over and
over.

"Do you think he meant it?" my mother asked. "Who is
this man?"

"I don't know. . . . Do you think they want to steal my idea?
Make me sign a paper, then don't pay me? How do we know
they will keep their word?"

"You saw the man. How did he look—honest?"

"He looked mean. Never smiled. I didn't like him."

For days my parents pondered the offer. They were not famil-
iar with the legal processes for protecting patents. They decided
to follow their feelings and reject the offer.

The bestselling of the products and services offered by D.
Kwon & Co. was the bamboo draperies. The draperies were
gaining favor with the people of the islands. The limitless colors
and sizes and the numerous purposes served by the woven bam-
boo for home and commercial decor provided our employees
with work all-year round. Upholstery services, originally the
only line offered, were gradually being phased out. Since the
shop could handle just so many orders and since the bamboo
drape was an exclusive, it took precedence over requests for
other goods and services.

My father began to take a closer look at his money-making

product. How could he improve it? An answer came one day when a particularly poor shipment of bamboo material arrived. He cursed the manufacturer in Japan. The lack of consistency in the quality of his shipments was noticeable. At times the slats of bamboo were rough and splintery and the weaving uneven. At other times the bamboo was choice and smooth, as if special care had been taken in selecting the fibers. The fact that the Japanese supplier was not more interested in fine craftsmanship was disturbing.

In all the years my father was in business he believed in turning out only the best product he was capable of. Obviously the Japanese merchant did not share the same attitude.

A friend visiting our family one day suggested, "Mr. Kwon, why don't you make a trip to the Orient? Find out for yourself who makes the best-quality material for your needs."

My mother agreed the suggestion was worth thinking about. "This will be your first trip on a boat since you were a boy, won't it? I think you should go."

Although he could afford better accomodations on the ship, my father traveled by third-class steerage. Most Koreans from Hawaii were still traveling third class in the 1930s, as if they knew of no other travel space on board. So my father journeyed to the bamboo manufacturing centers in Nara, Nagasaki, Kyoto, and Osaka.

He returned triumphantly from his trip after having established a relationship with Miyoshi Bamboo Factory, a modest firm headed by a superb craftsman named Miyoshi. A humble man, almost subservient in attitude, he had escorted his new client from Hawaii on a tour of other, larger bamboo firms in the country.

When the first rolls of the bamboo from his company reached our shop, the employees were ecstatic. They hailed it as absolutely perfect material. Incredibly clean were the bamboo slats and devoid of splinters, and the weaving was unbelievably even. One step in production could be eliminated—the singeing with a blow torch—because the bamboo arrived practically free of loose fibers.

Besides these advantages, some rolls of the new order had a self-design never seen before: the knots, or nodes, in the natural bamboo plant appeared in a pleasing pattern, as if in one movement the fat bamboo poles had been sliced by machine and immediately, in the next movement, the weaving had occurred. So when the material was cut and hung on a window it looked like bamboo trees were actually growing in a room, with the tree joints delicately swelling at regular intervals.

However, this pattern was discontinued when the "scattered nodes" pattern was developed; the knots or joints of the bamboo stalk, instead of being placed together, were artfully distributed all over the woven material so that they resembled the tiny bumps in lovely shantung silk.

We moved again. In January, 1937, we left the dusty, noisy factory premises for our former home on Nehoa Street. The coconut tree planted in the front yard had grown and now grass covered almost the entire lot. The healthy avocado tree in the back was so tall it was beginning to shade the rooms in the back of the house in the afternoon.

The shop still built custom furniture, but we were like the cobbler's family who went without shoes. My father often drove his customers to our house to show a sample of a certain chair or table. Before we knew it the chair and table disappeared.

"Yobo, where do you expect our guests to sit—on the floor?" my mother complained.

"I can't help it. We just can't seem to fill custom orders fast enough," was his sheepish reply.

CHAPTER 13

Poinciana

DURING the spring and summer the pink, gold, and rainbow shower trees came into bloom. These tall trees grew in the older residential sections of the city, especially in Makiki and Manoa. The golden showers, glistening in the sun, hung in clusters like yellow grapes. The pink shower trees were laden thick with blossoms; their branches resembled long carnation leis. And the rainbow showers took your breath away, for their masses of tiny peach and white and pink flowers crowded for a place in the sun, and their fulness even hid the green leaves of the tree.

Then there were the poinciana trees, which appeared in regal glory in the summer and lasted through fall. Many of them lined the streets in Makiki. The royal poinciana, as they were sometimes called, did not grow as large as the shower trees. But they stood proudly, spreading their branches like umbrellas decorated with fiery red and orange flowers.

One July afternoon my father came home and told us he had been strolling under poinciana trees on Wilder Avenue.

"You went walking on a hot day like this? Why?" my mother wondered. The temperature was near ninety degrees for the fourth day in a row and everybody complained of the humidity.

I recognized the odor of perspiration drying off his shirt and face—that "peculiar *man smell* of your father" as my mother referred to it. When he was inspired he usually was oblivious to fatigue and heat.

"Today I found a name—a good name!" he announced.

Mother cried, "What name? What are you talking about?"

"Poinciana! That's what I'm going to call it!" He sat down at the round kitchen table, his hands folded in front of him. He moved his lips as if talking but made no audible sounds.

Busy preparing dinner, we ignored him. Mother placed a pan on the stove and poured oil into it. I stood by to help fry the fish.

Suddenly my father jumped up. "Yes, that's what I'm going to call it!"

"Call who—what?" I asked. The oil heating in the pan started to sizzle and spatter.

He spoke in a hushed voice, one hand outstretched, palm moving away. "Can't you see it? P-O-I-N-C-I-A-N-A Bamboo Draperies. How do you like it?" His eyes were shining as if he'd seen a phantom.

Mother slid a whole fish into the hot pan and for a moment she was distracted by the sputtering contact of fish and oil. The word poinciana was foreign to her. She muttered, "I can't see anything good about that name."

But the word was registered legally as a tradename. Soon Poinciana caught on in households in Hawaii, and the mere mention of the word was associated with the popular type of window treatment using woven bamboo.

During the latter years of the 1930s there was a building boom. While the venetian blind dealers in town chopped prices lower and lower in the stiff competition for orders, D. Kwon & Co. sold the Poinciana Draperies at high enough prices to cover costs of production with a reasonable profit. People visiting our showroom fingered with longing the sample bamboo displays. But they shook their heads and said that ordinary venetian blinds combined with inexpensive side hangings of cloth were much cheaper for their windows.

Once a year D. Kwon & Co. held an anniversary sale. The response was amazing. I was attending college then but was able to help at the shop some afternoons and on Saturdays. I can still remember the first days of a sale when customers rushed into the store and lined up to place their orders. Housewives beseeched me to take the money in their hands as down payment for an order. Such clamoring of voices, each woman waving a wad of bills or a check, anxious to take advantage of the sale prices! Some of them recounted how long they had hung sheets or old, worn drapes on windows, and put aside money each month until they could afford to buy the beautiful bamboo draperies.

My father was an inventor who was not concerned with streamlining production of goods to reduce costs. He was unlike Henry Ford, who was obsessed with the idea of mass producing so that more people could afford to buy his product. Many new homes were being constructed but most of the owners purchased Poinciana Draperies only for their living rooms and dining rooms—"their best rooms in the house," as they were referred to.

In 1937 a young tenor named Kim Soo Han arrived from Korea to raise money for his people suffering under Japanese oppression. He reported in grim detail the excessive acts of cruelty perpetrated on his countrymen. Japan's ambitious warlords had stepped up military exploitation in Korea, as well as in neighboring Asian countries. The slim singer, always dressed neatly in a dark suit, roused the Korean immigrant community, especially the women who flocked around him with money and gifts. They admired his romantic voice. They adored his winsome smile and youthful ardor. At times they treated him as their own son or brother, at other times as the idol of their dreams. He was feted everyday with elaborate dinners at the homes of the women. He basked in their favor and love.

From the pulpit of the Methodist church he described how Christians were treated in his homeland: They were ferreted out at night from secret meeting places, which were usually in homes; they were punished for not worshipping the emperor, whom the Japanese considered divine; they were provided a despised "godstand" before which they were to worship. The Shinto religion was forced on all Koreans.

The congregation wept when Kim related that recently one

Methodist minister had been dragged to prison and flogged and, when he refused to profess Shintoism, a mixture of red pepper and water was poured into his nostrils, a sharp instrument poked relentlessly under his cuticles, and a pointed stick pushed into his ear.

My mother remembered well the independence march of 1919, and the old revolutionary spirit in her was revived. How she longed for her country to be free. How she wished the Japanese could be overthrown.

She invited the singer often to our house. Together with a group of her close friends they listened to him and laughed and sang with him. Mr. Kim was a showman; his black hair slicked down, he flashed his teeth when speaking or laughing. He had the strange habits of noisily drawing in the mucous in his nose when he ate peppery-hot kim chee and making loud, slurping sounds when he enjoyed noodles. I used to stare at him in disbelief; I wondered if it was the latest custom in Korea to act so primitive and crude.

One day when my father came home from work he saw the table set again for several guests. He knew who the guest of honor would be. His anger was rising when he asked me, "Where is your mother?"

"Up there," I replied, pointing to a group of ladies across the street. "She's taking pictures of Mr. Kim."

He looked out the window. On the steps of the new Roosevelt High School was the singer in his dark suit. He was grinning, facing the sun, while a number of women in Korean dress urged him to put on a bigger smile. Then each of them took turns posing with him. We could hear their laughter.

"Damn him," my father uttered under his breath. "I'm sick of seeing him around here." He stalked out of the house, rushed to his truck, and roared out of the driveway. He did not return home until late at night.

The next morning he made his own breakfast and was gone before the rest of the family was up.

At dinnertime he returned home. There was a tension in the air. We all sat down to eat, no one saying a word. Halfway through the dinner my father began to draw attention to himself by dropping his chopsticks emphatically, gulping water noisily, and spooning his soup as if he were shoveling it. He cleared his throat several times.

Then he bellowed, "I don't want to see that flat-faced singer around here again!"

"Mr. Kim?" Mother's voice was hardly audible. Then she spoke, defending him, "He is giving us news about our people."

"I don't care. You're just as bad as the rest of those crazy women. You all think he's a god!"

"No we don't. What are you saying?" She tried to remain calm.

"Why do you invite him here so often? Are you in love with him?" The spoonful of soup he held in his hand suddenly was hurled in her face. My brothers, sister, and I gasped. We had never seen our parents behave this way before.

"Remember, I don't want that damn singer around here again. And I don't want you hanging around that parasite!"

All was quiet after that outburst.

Kim Soo Han remained in Honolulu a few weeks longer, giving more benefit concerts and speeches. My mother attended several of the events where he spoke. She confided in me that he rekindled the revolutionary fervor and zeal she had felt as a young woman ready to fight against Japanese aggression. "When I hear Mr. Kim I know conditions are worse now, much worse," she sighed. "So many more Koreans are reduced to poverty. The Japanese are taking from our people their land, their money, and, worst of all, their dignity. They're cutting up our beautiful country for their military needs. They're building railroads and industrializing the economy for their military purposes. They're invading and exploiting other countries, too. Oh, they're awful, terrible!"

I listened with rapt attention, not so much because I felt sorry for the suffering in Korea but because this was the first time my mother openly revealed her feelings about the plight of her people. Heretofore she was like most of the older people I knew, who did not say much to us of the younger generation about their frustration and their desire for independence. It seemed as if our immigrant parents felt apologetic and ashamed of the status of their people, of themselves who were "a people without a country." I personally had never said I was proud to be a Korean because the feeling had not been instilled in me.

Mother lamented, "The women are suffering so much. Oh, so much. In some some rural areas I hear that innocent women on the way to the market are stopped by the police and taken in for questioning. These women might be the wives of men suspected to be spies or working against the imperialist government. At the station, I hear the women are stripped naked, jeered at by the officers, slapped, bruised, shamed, and interrogated for hours about related and unrelated happenings in the community. *Ai gu!*"

After the tenor's departure from the islands, I noticed the parishioners gathered each Sunday with renewed energy and unabashed vociferation for their country's imperative need for freedom. They cursed the loathsome, frenzied activities of the Japanese. The perpetrators of suffering were labelled "crazed people." The men swore at the *weh-num,* the spiteful enemy. The women wept, holding hands, and decried the state of affairs in their homeland.

In the midst of this fever and furor against the enemy one of the parishioners announced his daughter was marrying a young man of Japanese ancestry. He said the couple had met at a mainland college and they were very much in love. This impending marriage provoked an uproar in the Korean community. The wedding, which was to be quiet and private, became a public issue. The handsome aunt of the bride, a staunch Christian and an influential leader in the church, was unable to dissuade the bride from "the unforgivable act of bending to serve the enemy." She refused to sanction the marriage. The church people disapproved the use of the church for the wedding ceremony. "This is a traitorous union," the vocal members in the community declared.

The wedding took place in the bride's parents' home with

only a few members from the bride's and groom's families present.

My girlfriends and I were aware of the strong anti-Japanese feeling in the community, especially in regard to intermarriage. We agreed the prudent thing to do was to avoid dating Japanese boys. And even if we were invited to a dance or a movie by a Chinese or Caucasian, perhaps we should keep the relationship from turning serious. We were suddenly conscious we were a small minority among the races in Hawaii.

When I graduated from the University of Hawaii, jobs were scarce; for women, jobs were almost nonexistent. I could have ventured as a teacher to the outer islands—Maui, Kauai, or Hawaii—as did some of my friends who graduated with me. But my father was adamant that I not subject myself to "fighting in a classroom with kids who don't want to learn." He had heard the status of a public school teacher was degrading. He suggested I become an interior decorator, but neither he nor I knew where I could go for training.

The situation confused and disappointed my mother. "At least you have finished college. I am pleased for that." She added, "I guess there really are no jobs for women. Perhaps you will find something to do later. For now you can stay with us in our business."

In the fall I began to manage the office at D. Kwon & Co. Working and dealing with people in the business world was more difficult than working for a degree and with professors. Somehow I expected pure bliss outside of the classroom, with no pressures of exams and papers due. But the nine-to-five job proved tiring, and pleasing customers was demanding.

My evenings, however, were free. Soon I met and fell in love with a young man of Korean ancestry. Before we could announce our engagement, a sudden, unexpected event occurred that forced us to delay it.

One Saturday night my fiancé and I were driving around with some friends, trying to decide what we should do. Passing the Waikiki Theatre on Kalakaua Avenue, we noticed a long line of people waiting to buy tickets for the late show, featuring the popular stars Betty Grable and Tyrone Power. We hardly expected the film, *A Yank in the R.A.F.,* would be the very last evening showing we would see that year and for a long time after that.

The next morning, Sunday, December 7, 1941, I was awakened by the news that Japan had bombed Pearl Harbor. Joseph B. Poindexter, Governor of the Territory of Hawaii, proclaimed the islands in a "defense period." Later that day he placed the territory under martial law and called on the people to obey the federal military authorities.

By nightfall our family was separated and scattered. My eighteen-year-old brother, Young Mahn, who was enrolled in the Reserve Officers Training Corps (ROTC) class at the University of Hawaii, responded to a radio call for all ROTC men to report to the armory. We did not hear from him for over a week. We were worried. Finally he called from a beach in Kahuku and informed us he was part of the Hawaii National Guard, keeping watch on the beaches of the island.

My younger brother, Young Chul, left home the day of the attack to join other fifteen-year-old Boy Scouts of Troop 11 reporting to the Royal Hawaiian Hotel as "trained litter bearers." (The young boys had received training only the summer before at camp.) The scouts dined on superb food prepared by the chefs of the famous hotel. During the night the boys stayed beside their stretchers on the lawn of the hotel, close to the army ambulances, nervously waiting for the return assault of enemy planes. After the first night the litter bearers were divided into shifts and took turns going home to sleep and returning for duty to the hotel. The scouts were kept on this schedule for two weeks.

My father joined volunteer truck drivers, taking his own company vehicle to the Civil Defense Headquarters set up at Iolani Palace and awaited orders from the military. Dozens of men brought their trucks and blankets, and waited night after night for some assignment of duty.

At home my mother, sister, and I took care to leave no light burning. Occasionally we heard army trucks rumbling past our house in the pitch-black night, probably making their way up to Makiki Heights, which was above our home. Everyone in Hawaii waited in terror for the return of the Japanese. We lived that way for days, alert and afraid, families separated, schools closed, businesses shut down except for the grocers' and the druggists'.

When businesses were permitted to reopen, they were ordered to close promptly at 4:30 P.M. At that time blackout in California was also in effect because the navy hinted sighting bombers near there. As the fear and hysteria of the possible return of Japan's war planes diminished, businesses were allowed to operate for longer hours. But everyone had to be off the streets by sundown. According to a police report: "in December 1941 Honolulu's crime was cut to an all-time low."

From time to time grocers were asked to prepare inventories of their food supplies. The university offered advice through the newspapers on how to prepare food: "Do not allow food to be wasted. Eat a little less than usual. Conserve fats. Boil, stew or bake food instead of frying."

The full impact of war with Japan did not dawn on my father until he learned that all trade between the United States and Japan was cut off. In the immediate reaction of protecting the islands from further attack by Japan, he had not thought of the economic effect of the war. No longer could he import bamboo. No longer could he sell Poinciana Draperies. His big money-maker was doomed.

CHAPTER 14

Romantic Spring of '42

AFTER Japan's surprise attack on Pearl Harbor, followed by the declaration of war by President Roosevelt, blackout in Hawaii was stringently observed. Curfew hours were set by martial law. Restaurants and theatres opened their doors for business again but were ordered to close before sunset.

We found ourselves sitting at home in the dark night after night. A family needed at least one blacked-out room in the house for a meal or a game of cards, or for reading or sewing. Without such a room the only other alternatives were to sit and chat with one another in the dark, or go to bed.

To keep light from filtering out at night some people painted their windows black; but that cut off air circulation in the room and brought stuffiness. Besides, during the day, windows painted black looked ghastly, especially from the outside. Some people nailed heavy fabrics over windows to shut out light, but the effort was not satisfactory or attractive.

My father was challenged to devise more than one kind of blackout curtains or shades. In big demand was a product that could darken a lighted room completely from the outside as well as provide ventilation inside. To serve this purpose he found heavy denim and khaki the most suitable fabrics to use. A popular model he sold was the snap-on-curtain, which covered a window by snapping it on the wall or frame around the window. During the day these curtains could be tied back to the sides or be removed altogether. The snaps, strong and heavy, resembled those used in awning and sailing equipment.

In the early months of 1942, blackout curtains became an important line at D. Kwon & Co. The Honolulu Academy of Arts invited my father to enter the Academy's "Exhibit of Blackout Curtains." The story about the four guest exhibitors was carried by *The Honolulu Advertiser* on April 21, 1942. It said: "The exhibits offered by Dorothy True Bell [an interior decorator] and D. Kwon show overlapping black draperies set forward from venetian blinds so that night air can circulate in the rooms but no light can penetrate outside." The Hawaiian Electric Co. displayed a model suitable for a kitchen, and the Academy showed a room "using a removable slot ventilator . . . perfected in England."

One evening the U.S. Navy honored my father at a dinner for "his gift of blackout curtains at the Naval Hospital in Aiea."

Business in general was booming in Hawaii. People were buying almost everything in sight. The merchandise that disappeared fastest, I noticed, were refrigerators, washing machines, and cars—either new or used; goods with metal parts would become scarcer and scarcer as the war continued. New toys for children made of wood, rubber, and paper appeared on the market. Because priority shipment space was given to military and food supplies, retailers of general goods had to wait and wait for their merchandise from the mainland to fill their shelves.

My father hired a young, capable seamstress, so my mother was relieved of her work at the factory. She then found time to devote to community work. Like many other Koreans she joined in wholeheartedly to support the efforts of the United States to defeat Japan. How she and her compatriots hoped and prayed they could realize by the end of the war their dream of freedom from Japanese rule! A large number of Korean women volunteered daily at the Red Cross. With them my mother devoted hours and hours to rolling bandages. She also made contacts from house to house selling U.S. War Bonds. She was lauded for her unusual salesmanship, for her amazing success in compelling Koreans to buy bonds regularly by the week or by the month. In our family alone each of us children owned numerous twenty-five-dollar bonds; our parents bought them in larger denominations.

My younger brother and sister attended high school. Besides the regular curriculum, they were taught how to help during the war. They learned to use gas masks in case of enemy attack; then, in turn, they taught their neighbors how to wear the masks—those ugly, grey-green contraptions that made everyone look like inhabitants from another planet. My brother and sister learned how to save by buying war stamps, and they filled booklets with them.

They learned, too, how to pick the fruit in the pineapple fields when the field laborers were drafted into the army or left for better-paying defense jobs. Picking pine, the youngsters discovered, was back-breaking work. But they enjoyed the free bus ride from school to field, singing merrily all the way. At noon they sat in the red dirt and ate picnic lunches under a blazing sun. At the end of the day, feeling totally weary, they were ready for bed. The small wages they received in compensation added to their satisfaction.

Our family was adjusting well to war-time living when suddenly a stark letter from my brother Young Mahn arrived one morning, notifying us he had been shipped out to "somewhere in the Pacific" with the 298th Infantry. The letter hit Mother hard. She took to her room and began sobbing and beating her breast. "My son, my son, you're gone forever! I've lost you!" she wailed. "You, my first-born-son—I've lost you—what shall I do?" She cried unashamedly.

Her voice was hoarse by the time Father came home from work. Her wailing continued. It was so unlike her to weep and moan aloud. She reminded me of a professional weeper hired by some wealthy families to perform at funerals.

Father went into the room but came out almost immediately. Throwing up his hands in resignation, he said, "Ahhh-hh— your mother absolutely refuses to be comforted."

Then I went into the room and softly asked, "Omoni, what

can I do for you?" She broke into a fresh torrent of anguish, louder than before.

We moved about in the house as quietly as possible so our mother would not be further disturbed. None of us understood why she was so distressed, acting as if her son were already dead.

After what seemed like an interminable time her sobbing was barely audible. When I peeked in the room, I saw my mother still sitting on the floor where I had last seen her, her head bowed, her body shaking with soft sobs. She looked exhausted. I called for help, and with my father lifted her to her bed.

We never asked why she had indulged in hysterical weeping that day for fear she might start all over again. I wondered whether it was a custom practiced in Korea to yield to prolonged weeping when the death of someone dear was believed imminent.

Spring in 1942 was marked by a profusion of flowering romances in the islands. In fact, it was a season for weddings everywhere in America as young men married their girls before going off to battle. The couples who found it difficult to meet in the evenings in areas where blackout was enforced decided it was easier to be together if they were married.

Since my fiancé Philip and I had been planning to be married before the outbreak of World War II, we agreed that spring of '42 was a good time for our wedding. Although Philip and I knew that my mother favored ceremonies and formalities, we had no go-between to arrange a betrothal as was the custom in the old country. We were aware that she disapproved of Philip primarily because he lacked a college degree. But it was common knowledge that most young men of Korean ancestry his age had dropped out of college during the Depression to help support the family.

Some of my friends told me that no matter what the circumstance, mothers are never pleased with the choice of spouse their son or daughter makes.

I thought it was important to marry a Korean, not a Japanese or any other nationality, to avoid the wrath of the Korean community and escape bringing embarrassment to my family. To my surprise, I learned that to my mother nothing mattered more than a college degree held by the man or woman any of her children married. She had not made that wish clear to me.

Despite how she felt about her prospective son-in-law, my mother plunged into elaborate preparations for my wedding in May. Her friends were excited.

"You must give a big reception for your first-born child," they suggested.

"How can I? This is war time."

"Oh, that's right," they regretted. "We're disappointed. Then you'd better plan on a nice ice cream and cake party for the reception. But when your first son gets married, Hee Kyung, remember—you must give a big *jan-che!* Promise us. Of course, we'll help you."

My wedding was planned to take place at the Korean Methodist Church on a Sunday afternoon at two o'clock. One evening before the occasion my father was asked to help address about 250 invitations.

After stuffing the first dozen or so envelopes he complained, "This is too much like work. It's boring."

After a while, however, he seemed to be enjoying the task. Holding up an envelope he remarked, "This lady, Mrs. Sin Dok Lee, is very fat. So I wrote her name b-i-g." He showed us the guest's name and address scrawled in large, swollen letters covering the entire width of the envelope.

My mother glared at him. Chuckling, he picked up another invitation. "Now Mr. and Mrs. Cho, being such short people, especially Mrs. Cho—she's small like a mouse—I wrote their names small." The writing on the envelope was infinitesimal and almost illegible.

"For heaven's sake, behave yourself. Stop this nonsense!" my mother scolded. "I can't be re-doing all your—" She shook her head.

On the invitations to people he personally liked and respected, we noted his best penmanship. When the envelopes were stacked in neat piles late that night I heard my mother sigh, "I know some people will be unhappy when they receive their invitations. They will feel insulted by your father's handwriting. I wonder if I should reorder and redo some of these."

"I forbid you to do that!" my father snapped in a loud voice.

On the night of the wedding rehearsal at the church we waited and waited for my father to show up. Pacing up and down the aisle was my mother, who was in charge of the rehearsal. "Where is this man? Don't tell me he forgot he's supposed to be here tonight."

When he finally showed up, she pushed him into line behind the maid of honor as the party was progressing toward the chancel. Everyone was keeping time to the music except the father of the bride. He kept turning around and falling out of line.

"What do I do with my hands?" he asked helplessly.

"Don't worry about your hands! Your daughter will be walking beside you. She'll be holding your arm. She's not in line now because we hear it's bad luck for the bride to practice before the wedding."

All of a sudden she put her hands on her hips and burst out, "I don't see why you have to be in this wedding procession at all. What have *you* done for your daughter? *I'm* the one who should be taking her up the altar!" One of my parents was feeling luckier than the other.

After the ice cream and cake reception at the church parish hall, a sit-down dinner for about forty close friends and relatives was planned. I noted with disbelief the extravagant motions my mother went through preparing the dinner. The day before the wedding, six of her women friends came to the house to help with the chopping and the frying and the boiling of beef, pork, chicken, fish, and a variety of vegetables—in quantities to serve at least a hundred people or more.

I knew the custom was for a Korean hostess to express in a sing-song manner to guests seated at a table laden with food:

"I'm so sorry. There is so little for you to eat." The guests then respond in a chorus, reassuring her politely, "Oh, there is enough."

Not all the women who came to help that day went home before the curfew. I guessed those who remained would spend the night at our house.

Why did I not plan to spend the eve of my wedding at a hotel as some of the recent brides I knew had done? I could have been spared a sleepless night of tossing and turning.

Ah—the sounds and smells of wedding preparations! My bedroom was on the south side of the house and the large avocado tree stood just outside my window. At about ten o'clock the women decided to move out of the kitchen and sit under the avocado tree to fry the fish and meat in pans set on charcoal braziers. At first they kept their voices low. But these women of Kyungsangdo, excitable by nature, soon forgot the sleeping neighborhood and engaged in spirited conversation.

I put my head under the blanket to escape the chattering as well as the aroma of fish cooking. It was a losing battle.

The women began by telling stories about brides and grooms. I listened. I recognized the voice of a Mrs. Kim. "If we were living in Korea our spouses would be much younger than we are. We would become old and grey; then our husbands would leave us and look for concubines."

"Yeah," Mrs. Lee agreed. "Not like us over here. Our husbands—most of them—are so much older. They sent us pictures of themselves as young men, and when we came to Hawaii to marry them we found they were old, old men."

The tiny Mrs. Cho then began teasing my mother. "Say, Hee Kyung, didn't your husband immigrate when he was only seventeen, or was he sixteen?"

"Seventeen. I married him when he was twenty-four and I was eighteen."

Laughing, Mrs. Cho continued, "But didn't he ever tell you he ran away and left a wife and child behind?"

"Don't be silly. That's not true," my mother countered.

"How do you know? Boys are betrothed when they're very,

very young, you know. Perhaps your husband was to marry a twenty-seven-year-old hag? And he didn't like her looks, so he left Korea in a hurry?" The women broke into tittering and gig-gling.

I felt embarrassed for my mother. To think my father could have done a thing like that! No. He couldn't have.

Mrs. Chun spoke next. "Hee Kyung, you don't know how happy I am for you because your daughter is marrying a Korean boy." She sounded wistful. I knew she had been feeling ashamed because her only daughter recently had chosen a Japanese for a husband, who forced a pregnancy on her, besides. A hush fell over the group, as if Mrs. Chun were crying and the other ladies were in sympathy.

Somehow I finally drifted off to sleep.

The next morning when I woke up the first thought that came to my mind was "where will I sleep tonight? Will my father have delivered the bed he promised for our bedroom?"

Philip and I had found a charming furnished cottage in Makiki, not far from my parents' home. It was set back from the street, nestled among low plumeria and breadfruit trees. We had asked the rental agent to remove the furnishings from the tiny bedroom because we were receiving a bedroom set as a gift from my father.

I went over to the cottage to arrange the furniture. But none of it was there. I knew the shop worked from one deadline to the next in deliveries, but just this once couldn't it have been different? Was I to be like a cobbler's child even on my wed-ding day?

The bedroom and bathroom in the cottage were both very small. And the cooking area I called my postage-stamp kitchen. However, the living room and dining room could accomodate thirty or more people. Thick *lau hala* covered the floors. Just outside the large screened front door was a spacious, aged brick patio under an enormous, old koa tree—a romantic place to dance and enjoy drinks.

At twelve noon, two hours before the wedding, my father and a young man brought the bedroom pieces to the house, the paint on them barely dry. As he started to leave the apartment I called, "Abuji, you're not forgetting the wedding, are you? You must go home now and wash up. Put on your white suit."

"Oh, that's right. I'll go home now," he replied.

There was hardly time for me to throw a spread over the mattress and display the beautiful *ibul* on the bed.

The rest of the day rushed by more quickly than I would have wished. The wedding ceremony and reception at the church were followed by the visit of some of the guests to the bridal cottage.

I was in the midst of opening gifts and sipping a drink when someone reminded me and Philip that we had dinner guests waiting at my parents' home. I remember wading through what seemed like endless puffs of tissue paper looking for my shoes. Everyone was picking up balls of soft paper and moving gift boxes, trying to help me find my white satin shoes.

My new husband and I hurried to the dinner, for the guests would have to leave for their homes before the eight o'clock curfew.

CHAPTER 15

Old Men and Ladies' Handbags

As the war continued it seemed almost every able person in Hawaii chose to work in defense jobs. Ice cream vendors no longer annoyed mothers by luring children to their singing vehicles and tempting them just before dinnertime. Door-to-door salesmen with brushes, encyclopedias, and carpet sweepers vanished from sight. Even the cruising neighborhood vegetable man, whom we had depended on for years, found other employment.

The scarcity of goods in the islands became more and more apparent. Although no one went hungry, food—especially fresh vegetables and meat—was in short supply.

As a new bride I joined other housewives struggling to find and buy groceries. At one time I saw a pregnant woman who yearned for bacon going from store to store, begging for a pound or at least a half pound. The grocers shook their heads and told her that they would be lucky if they received an allotment of such luxuries as bacon and ham. When the woman cried, "How come, all of a sudden, bacon is so hard to find?" the butcher replied, "Lady, we're at war! The army and navy get their share first."

To find fresh vegetables and meat was often a matter of running from market to market. When I heard that lettuce and cabbage were expected at a certain store at two o'clock, I excused myself from the office. I found a line already formed outside that store when I got there. There were no supermarkets in Honolulu then; we were at the mercy of arrogant, independent butchers and insolent clerks with whom we had to "try and make friends." It was easy to understand why many people took up cultivating "victory gardens" in their backyards.

I stood in many ration lines for needed items. Gasoline was rationed. Like a fool, I also stood in the liquor line for a week's quota of Scotch or bourbon. My husband and I and our friends became "straight drinkers"; we rationalized there was little time to sip highballs before blackout, so we drank from jiggers, some expensively etched by artists. Our liquor supply grew each week.

My father lost his employees one by one either to the draft or to defense jobs. As a result, he found himself free from the pressure of running the factory. He still had the rental income from the two cottages next to the factory; the third cottage was filled with scrap pieces of bamboo. He also received income from the former D. Kwon & Co. showroom, which was converted into a lucrative pool hall by a lively, lean woman, who operated the amusement hall day and night. For many defense workers who worked on night shifts, playing pool was a way of spending the day with friends. Pool halls sprouted up all over the city.

The monolithic shop-and-factory stood idle day after day. No sounds of hammering or painting or sewing. The partial rolls of unsold bamboo leaning against the wall concerned my father. He felt perhaps he should be doing something with them. He had time on his hands.

Before long he became engrossed in a new patent idea. He experimented making women's handbags with split bamboo scraps, bits of string leather, and slats of wood. He was happy he could make use of odds and ends he found lying around the shop.

For decorative touches on the handbags, he added segments of bamboo poles and rattan. He discovered endless ways of combining materials. Whatever else he needed he could order from a wholesaler. The weeks he spent, undisturbed, creating in tactile form the ideas for women's purses gave him pure joy.

The first batch of the new handbags were on the market by the end of 1942, but the patent award for the invention was held up for more than ten years. Was it possible for a lady's bag to be so different in design and construction from those currently on the market or those manufactured in previous years to merit a patent? These were the questions the lawyers had to answer in their research and application for a patent. It is interesting to note that the four references specifically cited in my father's U.S. Patent No. 2,765,833 included the names of the men who had created similar types of handbags: Cohen, in 1953; Kuhlman, in 1949; and Elliott, in 1948.

It seemed people spent money freely during the war; whatever merchants displayed on their shelves sold. As the demand for his ladies' handbags grew, my father had to face the fact that if he worked alone, he could not produce enough to supply the retail outlets. Where could he go to find employees who were not already earning handsomely at Pearl Harbor or Hickam Field?

He thought of asking his friends, many of whom were retired men in their sixties. One day he asked two white-haired former Methodist ministers and a couple of former tailors if they wished to earn a little money by making ladies' purses. They thought my father was jesting. However, since they had great respect for "Mr. Kwon's smart mind," they agreed to try.

One morning the elderly men went down to the D. Kwon factory and began to stitch pieces of fabric and cord onto frames of purses. Their blunt, worn fingers slowly learned to sew by hand the flaps, buttons, and trimming onto woven bamboo. All the preliminary work of cutting, painting, and machine stitching on the bamboo was already done by my father.

Soon a few more members of the church—former launderers and shopkeepers—joined the workforce. The old men enjoyed the comradeship and the leisurely pace of the work. At noon they ambled down the street to a cafe, lunched together, and then went home in time for their afternoon naps.

The men appreciated the wages by-the-hour, and later by-the-piece completed at home. Years later, after the war ended, the men were also grateful for the Social Security stipends they began receiving, for my father had reported all their wages.

The handbags sold fast. Retail merchants, who had difficulty receiving merchandise from the mainland, eagerly bought island-made goods. To the casual eye the novel woven-bamboo bags looked easy to make. But no one made imitations, for the construction was intricate. The upper part of the bag was round and flexible, the lower part square and rigid. The mechanism for opening and closing was smooth and easy. The colors ranged from "natural" to other popular shades for bags.

Before long a variety of styles of women's handbags emerged from the old men's workshop. For the Fourth of July, in 1944, a patriotic design in an envelope style appeared, using red, white, and blue strips of wood. Each strip was laced to the next with matching red, white, and blue leather strips. These bags sold faster than the slow-moving cronies could produce them. But after Independence Day, interest in them diminished. However, the same style of purse made with half-inch strips of hardwood in a solid color sold the best; the natural-varnish finish with brown leather lacing was a favorite.

One day as my father and I were coming out of Liberty House department store, which was one of our retail outlets, we saw a dark-haired woman briskly walking by with one of our natural-varnish bags under her arm. My father stopped her and asked, "How do you like that purse?"

The startled woman drew back, clutching her purse tight. She formed her lips ready to scream. "I made that purse, you know," my father said.

"You—uh—what? Uh—excuse me. For a moment I thought you were going to snatch my purse." She tried to laugh.

"You like it?" my father asked again, smiling, totally unaware he had frightened her.

The woman, making an effort to calm herself, said, "Yes—I like it. In fact, I love it. It's strong." The woman then moved closer to us and whispered, "I own a bar in town. I carry cash receipts to the bank everyday in this purse. No one can tell I'm carrying so much money. It's the only purse that has held up. I love it!"

We were all pleased. She walked away, waving to us.

My mother received letters from my brother stationed in some desolate place in the Pacific. We guessed he was writing from the New Hebrides or somewhere in that area. He complained to her of his boredom and desire for some real action. But like all mothers with sons in the war she was glad he was not in a dangerous battle zone.

During the day she kept busy with volunteer work at the Red Cross and the sale of war bonds in the community. One day she revealed she had another interest that consumed some of her daytime hours. When she got home one day and flung her purse on the couch, it accidentally fell open, spilling hundreds of dollars to the floor.

"What's this?" I asked, surprised. "Why didn't you go to the bank? Why bring so much money home?" I counted the bills. There was over six hundred dollars.

"Oh, I don't know how much I have. I usually carry about five hundred dollars."

"What—! Why?"

"I might need that much some day. I might find a piece of property I like. I'll have the deposit ready. I want to buy for investment."

"Investment?" I asked. "What kind of investment?"

"I have friends who have bought rooming houses and are managing them. They're collecting rent. Making a good profit."

"You mean, like the rooming house Mrs. Kim bought on Hotel and Maunakea Street?" I shuddered. I had heard about those creepy, run-down rooms, occupied by pitiful old men, each one fending for himself. I could not imagine my mother going to such a place and demanding rent from poor men who used a community kitchen, ate alone in their rooms, did their own laundry, and for amusement merely looked out their windows at the passing parade of cars and people.

"Not only rooming houses," she added defensively. "I could buy a big, old-fashioned house and cut it up into small apartments. Mrs. Shon did that. She's just sitting down and getting rich."

The first piece of property my mother bought was an ancient, once-stately, Colonial-style mansion, located about three blocks from the family house. Every room in the large building was immense.

I asked, "Omoni, are you planning to divide this place into small units?"

She hesitated. "I don't think so—not right away—I think we'll move into it and live there awhile."

The gracious house sat in the middle of a large, level piece of land. On one side stood tall shower trees, which bloomed pink and yellow in the spring. On the opposite, sunny side of the house, the ground was flat and grassed, and bordered by a well-trimmed red hibiscus hedge. A ditch, with little or no water flowing in it except after a heavy downpour, divided the grounds of the house and the private driveway leading from the street to the large garage in the back. The chauffeur to the family living in the mansion might have occupied the unimposing quarters attached to the garage. And behind the great house was a low duplex cottage for, presumably, the servants.

The largest Pirie mango tree I had ever seen shaded the back lawn. Compared to it, the lichee tree standing near it looked weak and straggly. The real estate agent apologized that it had not borne any fruit in the six years since it was planted and might soon die. However, the year my parents moved in, and every year thereafter, the tree yielded luscious, plump lichees.

My mother believed she had found a bargain buying the whole property for sixteen thousand dollars in early 1944.

My father did not agree. "It looks like a useless museum," he said with disdain. "What are you going to do with such a big house? And so much yard to take care of. Who's going to mow the lawn? Me?"

Ignoring his questions, she spoke of numbers that impressed her. "Yobo, I feel guilty. We sold our Nehoa house for eleven thousand dollars. Imagine that! We paid only five thousand dollars for it ten years ago in 1931."

If my father was troubled by the yardwork demanded by the huge property, he was overwhelmed by the interior of the house. The ceiling of the first floor was twelve feet high. "I'm not climbing those stairs to get to the bedroom," he declared, pointing to the elegant staircase. "I'm sleeping somewhere downstairs—anyplace down here."

To his surprise Mother agreed. "That's a good idea. I think we'll make the living room our bedroom."

So the living room became the master bedroom; the enclosed lanai became the living room; and the dining room, with its polished *ohia* floor, became an enormous hall for entertaining. The pantry and kitchen were smaller and less impressive, with low ceilings and few windows. A room next to the kitchen housed a giant General Electric restaurant-model refrigerator.

On the opposite side of the house was the sun room, a room that appealed to family members and guests alike. It jutted out in a tall half-hexagon of beveled windows to catch all the light and sunshine possible.

On the second floor were three large bedrooms, and the third floor was an enormous attic.

The house was at least fifty years old. With occasional painting and repairing and termite treating, it was a comfortable home for my parents, my younger brother, and my sister.

"One more acquisition of property and my interest in business is satisfied," my mother said. The next purchase included two identical cottages sitting side by side on Prospect Street, with two units behind these cottages. Combined with the rentals collected from the dwellings behind the family's Colonial house, the latest property purchase provided a good income for my parents. However, they found being landlords involved more than "just sitting down and making money."

All her life my mother was devoted to her church. She had supported the Methodist church, together with a small, remarkably close-knit group of women, since they had first met as picture brides before 1920. This cadre of ladies included Mrs. W. K. Ahn, Mrs. W. L. Chung, Mrs. L. S. Lee, Mrs. B. S. Char, and my mother. They gave unstintingly of their time, energy, and money to keep their church running efficiently, building good relations between pastor and parishioners, and assuaging anger and dissatisfaction among the members as soon as such problems arose. They truly believed in the sanctity of the institution.

But about 1940 the cadre of ladies noticed the parishioners becoming restless, involved in petty quarrels, and expressing opposition to policies and personalities. Something ugly was emerging and spreading like a cancer, threatening the spiritual life and well-being of the church body.

The ladies were like well-meaning house repairmen, hurrying to fix a leaking roof here and replacing a termite-eaten board there, or planing rough spots in the building. Now the cancerous problem seemed ready to destroy the whole structure.

The ladies sighed when they located the vulnerable spot in the church—the source of the ailment. What could they do to remedy the problem of bilingual dissatisfaction? For the introduction of a bilingual minister had brought on a host of negative reactions.

For the sake of their children, the parishioners had requested the Methodist Headquarters to provide a minister who could preach in English for the young, as well as in Korean for the older people. At first, the suggestion was hailed as intelligent and appropriate. For the youngsters were ignoring their parents' native language and favoring the language they learned and used in the public school. They refused to attend the Sunday services unless the preacher could communicate with them.

There was the rub. Bilingual ministers came and went, some in a huff before their term was up, some with feelings of failure, others in near tears after receiving merciless criticism.

When a preacher spoke fluent English his Korean suffered, and he was ridiculed by the older members; when one preached in eloquent Korean, his English was weak. The diminishing number of young people in attendance disturbed the old-time members, who remembered the days when it was a custom for the whole family to attend church and worship together.

The church was changing its shape and form and appeal. The

new subdivisions developing outside of the city posed good reasons for members who had moved to drop their attendance. Most of the immigrants were no longer poor; some affluent people seemed to find the church superfluous in their lives.

The cadre of ladies continued to minister to each new pastor, comforting him and his wife, cheering them and promising unfailing support.

Our friends predicted that with the blackout nights in Hawaii Philip and I, like many other young marrieds, would soon be having babies. Twelve months after we were married I gave birth to our first child, a bright-eyed girl with a tremendous appetite for food and attention. We named her Merphil. Philip bought several boxes of cigars and chocolates to pass out to well-wishers, but the cigars remained almost untouched in the boxes. He heard such jibes as "You pass out cigars when you have a son!" or "I'll take one when it's a boy!" I wondered how much Philip wished we had a son as our firstborn. And I wondered how disappointed the baby's grandparents were. I knew that in Korea sons were a source of great pride since they carried on the family name.

Because my parents' house was so commodious, and because they wished us to be near them when our first child was born, my husband and I moved in with them. Our apartment-size quarters on the second floor included a large sitting room–bedroom, a bath, and a dressing room with a refrigerator for refreshments.

Merphil was an early riser—sometimes at six o'clock, often at five. As soon as she was able to sit up I found it convenient to take her downstairs to my father and mother, who at first did not appreciate being disturbed so early in the morning. But they could not resist entertaining their chubby, responsive grandchild; they even competed with each other for the chance to rock her on their stomachs while they lay in bed and engaged in baby talk.

After our second child, a son we named Garet, was born in 1944, my husband and I believed the Allies would need more men to win the war in the Pacific against Japan. Married men and some men with children were already being called into service. My husband said he was ready to join the armed forces.

Like other young wives, I was nervous and did not want him to go. I developed a terrible case of hives—big red splotches and welts appeared all over my body. The doctor, shaking his head, told me, "No amount of medicine or lotions will remove these splotches." "How can you say that?" I cried. "I must find relief. Please help me. I can't sleep at night for the itching." He looked at me and said very slowly, "You're upset over something. Whatever it is, you must stop worrying. . . ."

Our son was only two months old when my husband was called to combat duty. Toward the close of 1944 the global conflict of World War II was inexorably heading to a climax.

No sooner did my brother Young Chul turn eighteen in February 1945, but he too was called to serve. Now we had three men from our family in the U.S. Armed Forces.

CHAPTER 16

The Peace after Bombs

ATOMIC bombs were dropped on the industrial city of Hiroshima on August 6, 1945, and on the seaport town of Nagasaki three days later, killing over a hundred thousand people. This culminated the Allies' attempt to end World War II. Japan surrendered. Hitler's army had already admitted defeat in May 1945, and Mussolini had been driven from power in 1943.

My parents and their compatriots in Hawaii were jubilant beyond words when they learned of Japan's capitulation to the Allies. They rejoiced! They believed Korea would be freed at last of Japan's imperialist rule!

But an unexpected turn of events brought chagrin and anguish to Koreans, for communist Russia stepped in and claimed the northern half of their country. They had thought that when Russia entered the war against Japan, there was an agreement that she would defend the northern half of Korea while the United States defended the southern half until Japan was defeated. Another belief was that after a Korean government was formed, both Russia and the United States would remove their troops. But Russia insisted she had never agreed to such an agreement.

The United States proposed to set up a series of United States–Soviet Union Joint Commission meetings. Another U.S. proposal was to call a foreign ministers' conference with representatives from the United States, Britain, China, and Russia. Neither proposal was agreeable to Russia. A third proposal made was to present the case to the United Nations. The United Nations, in a Resolution, declared that after elections were held in Korea in 1947, the country would be unified and both the United States and Russian forces would pull out.

Russia adamantly refused to accept the U.N. Resolution. Instead, she set up a communist government at the 38th Parallel under the fierce leader Kim Il Sung. This was a crushing blow to all Koreans living in the native land as well as to those in other parts of the world. It marked another sad, sad day in their history.

So, the families who lived in northern Korea were permanently separated from their relatives in the south. This grieved my parents although both of them came from the south—Taegu and Andong.

The news of Syngman Rhee's election as President of the Republic of Korea met with mixed approval among the immigrant Koreans in Hawaii. There still remained a number of loyal supporters of Yongman Park, the man who originally opposed Rhee and who had planned to recapture his homeland from Japan by militaristic means. Park had been assassinated twenty years earlier, yet a vestige of his followers would have preferred to see a man other than Rhee heading their country. My mother and father and other Methodists greeted Rhee's ascension as head of their country with only mild enthusiasm.

Shortly after the war ended we welcomed home my husband and my brother with great joy. However, my younger brother, who was drafted a few months before V-Day, had to remain in the army to complete his basic training in Texas. After that, he reported to the Special Detachment Unit; in May, 1946 he was sent overseas as part of a replacement troop. Not until January, 1947, was he discharged from duty, almost two years after the war had ended.

Peacetime business activity began in earnest for businessmen after the war. Just when the U.S. government would permit resumption of trade with Japan was of great concern to my father. True, it would take time for Japan to rebuild her wartorn industrial cities. More than once he expressed distress and anxiety, for he feared he might never be able to manufacture Poinciana Draperies again.

Gradually the former employees of D. Kwon & Co. returned to their jobs as carpenters, painters, and upholsterers.

While my father waited for sea commerce to Japan's ports to open, he decided to turn his attention to construction of more rental units on his property. Architects and contractors, who were back from the service or war-related jobs, reopened their offices and they eagerly sought business. The building industry entered a postwar boom.

The old cottages next to the factory were torn down to make room for new buildings. A third cottage, filled with remnants of bamboo stored for years, had to be emptied of its contents. The waste was unbelievable: countless discarded pieces of split bamboo stacked from floor to ceiling in every room were piled up haphazardly, covered with dust, wound with spider webs, and smelled musty. For three whole days men from the shop hauled out truckload after truckload of scraps. And at the city dump, charges were incurred.

My mother, the practical one, threw up her hands in disgust as she watched. "What kind of stupid business is this?" Her hands on her hips, she turned to my father. "Didn't I tell you it was crazy to save all those scraps? You had enough of them in the shop. Boxes and boxes full! You know that every time you cut from a bamboo roll, there's bound to be something left over. And think of the loss of rent from that cottage all these years! *Ji-rral! Ji-rral!*"

My father—the dreamer, the experimenter, the artisan—said nothing.

A pair of twin shops was built on the other side of the driveway from the D. Kwon & Co. showroom. One of these small shops was rented for many years by Edward Hustace, a noted philatelist and coin collector; the other shop by K. Nagashima, a popular woman barber. Behind these shops went up an L-shaped, two-story apartment complex with parking stalls below. The dozen new apartments quickly filled with military and local families.

What should he do next? my father wondered. A restless person, he was at odds with himself unless something continually absorbed his mind and employed his hands. He still had no knowledge about U.S.-Japan trade relations.

Now that tourists were returning to the islands, the business-woman Elsie Krassas called my father to help her spruce up her Waikiki shop. He was fascinated by the display of the many innovative creations in her shop. Well-known as a designer, she revived the use of feathers in leis and hatbands. She made popular the muumuu, the holoku, and the sarong. Famous Hollywood stars like Dorothy Lamour, Bette Davis, and Bob Hope wore her colorful versions of traditional Hawaiian costumes and hats.

Her hats were ingenious inventions, using *lau hala,* coconut, palm, fern, and peacock feathers. My father observed her customers. How interesting and attractive they looked. He was convinced that a woman looked better-groomed, indeed, when she wore a hat to compliment her dress.

Hats fascinated my father; it wasn't long before he became a hatter himself. He artfully combined woven bamboo and grass matting to make pert, stylish hats. He spent hours trying to produce a marketable line of headdress. Many tourists who bought his hats said they were buying not only for themselves but for all the members of their bridge club back home. Matching bamboo handbags were available as well as other gift objects, such as place mats, coasters, and baskets.

In 1946 my parents heard of the Pan American Clipper service to the West Coast, and they felt the urge to travel.

My mother informed some of her Kyungsangdo friends of the trip she planned to take. They were more excited than she. They exclaimed, "To fly! To fly over an ocean! To cover miles and miles in a short time! To be able to afford such a trip!" The women talked about the flight as though it were a phenomenon.

In those days the Pan American Clipper followed erratic departure schedules. My parents went to the airport with a host of well-wishers. There they were informed the plane had engine trouble and could not take off until the next day. It was the same story the next day, and the next and the next.

The women friends were concerned. They called my mother with dire warnings: "Better not go, Hee Kyung. It's dangerous to fly by air. What if the engine of the plane fails in mid-air? You'll die! It's obvious a plane is not a dependable means of travel."

These intermittent phone calls made my parents jittery. They wondered whether the delay was an omen. Should they cancel the trip? They had friends in San Francisco and Los Angeles waiting for them. And my father planned to survey the business opportunities in the two cities.

Before they called off the trip, they heard that their plane was in perfect condition, ready to fly. They made the round trip across the Pacific and back without mishap.

Upon their return from the mainland my mother thought it was time to convert the large, old house the family lived in on Kewalo Street into small family rental units. This meant up-rooting her family and moving again.

They discussed the move. "This time let's live in a house that's not so old. That has no termites. A modern-looking place." She found just what they wanted—an attractive dwelling on Kakela Drive, behind Punahou School, not far from the Kewalo Street house. It was almost new, solidly built, and well-maintained.

The area was called Rocky Hill. Most of the houses in this area, although built on steep terrain, looked secure. Perhaps the abundance of rich, green foliage and trees gave the residences the appearance of being nestled close to the earth.

The family moved in. They discovered many of the neighbors were old-time residents, *kamaaina,* with names like Judd, Lowrey, Martin, Oakley, Halford, and Greenwell. Except for the Reverend Henry Judd, who came to call, these *kamaaina* families were not particularly receptive of newcomers in their neighborhood. They were people preoccupied with their lives, not bothering to wave or smile when they drove by.

In October of that first year my mother regretted losing the opportunity to gain favor with the children of the neighborhood. One night the doorbell rang, and Mother opened the door. She was confronted by seven or eight children, all about the same height, wearing grotesque masks and odd costumes. They shouted, "Trick or treat!"

She did not understand them. "What you say?" she asked.

"Trick or treat! Trick or treat!" the blond and red-headed youngsters repeated.

To my mother it sounded like "Truck! Truck!" She thought they wished to talk to her husband. She happened to be home alone.

She apologized, "My husband not home yet."

None of the children tried to explain what they wanted or why they were there.

"I can do something for you?" she inquired.

The children murmured again, "Trick or treat."

"I'm very sorry, very sorry," she said, perplexed, shaking her head.

She watched them retreat. They took their time. Bending their bodies, they backed toward the hedge on the side of the property. Then it was quiet. She assumed they had gone up the street.

The next morning my mother looked out and saw the front lawn littered with thousands of tiny pieces of newspaper. Later, with a rake in hand, she uttered, "How can anyone tear up newspaper into such small pieces?" She picked bits of paper clinging to the red torch ginger, the yellow chrysanthemums, in the stalks of panax, between blades of grass. She was embarrassed. She had to hurry and tidy the lawn before the neighbors drove past on their way to work.

That evening my sister and brother reported they had heard that many irate island residents had called radio stations and complained of nuisance tricks played on them the night before because goblins and ghosts had not been fed when they came by.

"All they wanted was a treat," Young Mahn said.

"What did they want?"

"Something like candy, Mama," Chung Hee explained.

"Oh, is that what they were saying. And I had a whole bowl full of beautiful apples and oranges on the table next to the door. I could have given each child one or two of them!"

CHAPTER 17

A Dirge for a Wedding

AT last my mother was able to look forward to a period of peace and prosperity when her younger son Young Chul was discharged from the army. He came home and resumed his college studies. The family was finally all united after World War II as she had hoped and prayed.

The dream of a college education for herself was replaced by a vow to see that all four of her children earned college degrees; one had succeeded, the three others were on their way.

After years of perseverence she and my father had achieved the good life. And she was happy her country had finally shaken off the yoke of Japanese tyranny by the Allies' efforts, particularly by the American move to drop atomic bombs on Japan. But she was sad that one of the results was the communist control of the northern half of her country.

Her friends praised my mother for her social concerns and for her amazing energy. She attributed her source of energy to eight or nine hours of sleep each night. She was lean, almost thin, for her five-foot height. Unlike some of her plump friends, she had never acquired a taste for pastries.

Her diet consisted mainly of soups, kim chee, and fresh vegetables. If it weren't for my father who insisted on seeing meat on the table she would not have served it. He was not satisfied with bits of meat sauteed with vegetables. His favorite dish was T-bone steak, and we had it often. After salting the meat it was a simple task to fry it on a high flame, cut it into small pieces for easy pick-up with chopsticks, and place the platterful in the center of the table. Boiled string beans and sliced ripe tomatoes almost always complemented the steak. My mother, however, took only occasional bites of the meat.

While my parents were involved with construction of rental units on their Beretania and Kewalo properties, my older brother Young Mahn approached them one day and stated he wished to marry his sweetheart before graduating from the university. "I've lost four years of schooling being away at war. Grace feels she's waited for me a long time," he said.

The announcement shocked my mother. "But you know how much it means to your father and me that you finish college—"

"Don't worry, Mama. I plan to continue school and get my diploma. And I'll keep working as I'm doing now for Abuji at the shop in the afternoons and on Saturdays, even after I'm married."

"What about Grace? What will she do?" my mother asked.

"She'll work as a nurse at Queen's Hospital. You know, she got her nursing degree while I was away."

The notion of their son's marriage caught both my parents by surprise. They needed time to plan a wedding according to Korean custom befitting a first son.

My mother suggested, "Let's think about this for a while. We have to consider repaying our social debts to our friends."

The wedding was scheduled for June. My parents realized they had only three months to prepare for the very special occasion. As her friends expected, they were called to help. Their enthusiasm and interest rose to a feverish pitch as the important day drew near.

"Hee Kyung, we're so glad you're planning a big *jan-che*," they exclaimed. "We think this will be the biggest *jan-che* since Pearl Harbor!"

"Yes—it's turning out that way, bigger than I anticipated," she agreed nervously. The growing guest list, including adults and children, was nearing one thousand. Usually in Korea the whole village was invited when a *yangban*'s son was married.

Neither of my parents knew of catering services at that time. Planning the giant celebration brought my mother many sleepless nights. She realized that despite the generous offer of help from her friends, only one person could hold together the strings of the whole *jan-che* operation.

It was planned the guests would attend the wedding ceremony at the church on Keeaumoku Street, then walk two streets over to the reception under the tent on the spacious grounds of the Kewalo Street house. A giant tent, the largest available, was rented for the wedding feast.

Since my father was not a social organizer, he discovered he was not much help in coordinating the countless tasks involved. My brothers and sister and I were disturbed, for the event appeared to us like a mammoth enterprise beyond sense or reason.

"Mama, why do you have to put on such a big, elaborate wedding? Why is tradition so important?" we asked.

She sighed, "In Korea it would be easier. The servants would run the errands and do much of the preparation. And there would be relatives. Here, we are the only Kwons."

The week before the wedding many different varieties of kim chee were ready, including cabbage, cucumber, radish, and onion. Spicy shredded codfish and aged pickled vegetables looked peppery red in huge crockery pots. Soda pop, ice cream, and cake—not traditional foods served at Korean weddings— were ordered for the happy event.

Two nights before the wedding, dozens of sizzling barbecue braziers lit up the lawn behind the big house. The ladies assisting in the cooking sat on mats on the grass and fried several kinds of *jhun*. They used smooth, long chopsticks to turn pieces of tender beef and fish fillet, which had been marinated in a special *kan-jang* sauce and dipped in egg batter. The aroma of the *jhun* permeated the homes of the neighbors, who peeked out of their windows; some of them couldn't help strolling over for a closer look and were rewarded with a sampling of the delicious meat and fish right off the stove. Lanterns and electric bulbs strung over the heads of the cooks lent a party atmosphere. There were chopping sounds—quick strokes of knives falling on the large pieces of the *jhun,* which was cut in countless squares and neatly arranged on decorative platters.

Inside the tent the men, under the supervision of my father, hammered together the buffet table tops on wooden horses and set up chairs in rows. Obviously the tent would not hold a thousand people at one sitting. The tables for the children were set up on the lawn where they would be free to roam and play in the yard.

The *namul* dishes to be made with zucchini, bean sprouts, watercress, and lily root remained as the last tasks for the morning of the wedding so that they would taste and look fresh. The *daak-chim*—chicken laced with bamboo shoots, gingko nuts, and mushrooms—also was saved for the last day of preparation.

But Korean sweets and delicacies were ready; the most popular of these included dark square pieces of *yak-kwa,* the layered *silu-dduk,* and the rich *yak-sik.* For the children there were sweet, chewy, oily cakes in bright green and pink.

The eve of the wedding day dawned bright and sunny. Reviewing all the preparations for the feast satisfied my mother that all was progressing according to schedule. She earnestly hoped, as Korean hostesses do, no one would go home hungry from the feast.

She proposed to my father, "Yobo, let's go down to the fish market to check with the *namul* suppliers and the poultry men."

Chinese and Koreans went to Chinatown and hand-picked live chickens for their dinners. The seller axed the chickens' heads, drained the blood, then wrapped the birds in newspaper. The buyer then returned home and dunked the birds in boiling water for easy removal of the feathers. It was believed that chickens slaughtered, dressed, and cooked the same day tasted superior to fowl brought to the table in any other way.

My parents drove their Buick sedan to the fish market on King and Kekaulike streets. Although the whole complex of individually owned stalls was called "the fish market," the popular market sold all kinds of food—pork and beef, canned foods, fresh vegetables, exotic foods from the Orient, as well as poultry and fish. The place was bustling with early-morning shoppers. After parking their car on King Street, my parents crossed over and came upon a crowd of people pushing to get close to the high-glassed counters and shout their orders to the men behind the counter: "One pound roast pork! Two pound short rib! I like mullet; gimme three!" Other shoppers were bending over vegetable and fruit stands to pick the choicest produce.

My parents made their way deep into one of the aisles and reached the Okada stall. Mr. Okada, a short, stout man with greying hair, greeted them. "Long time no rain," he worried, "but everything you order I can get for you."

The next stop for my parents was the noisy, smelly chicken stand far down on Kekaulike Street. In cages near the front entrance the ducks strutted about proudly, and brown hens cackled as if they were angry and scolding. The owner, a large Chinese man with a smooth, shiny face and black hair, came from the back of the shop. He grinned, revealing several teeth missing in his mouth. "I get your order. Anytime you like, I ready for you pickup."

"You sure—all number one, fresh chickens for me?" my mother asked.

"Yeah, yeah, Mrs. Kwon. You no worry. Numba one! All good! I guarantee."

She was absorbed in checking off the items on a list in her hand as she and Father made their way back to the car. They crossed King Street. Just before they reached the car she stopped. "Oh, I almost forgot," she said, "I must go back and ask Mr. Okada about the zucchini. It's important. He didn't tell me how much he could get. He said it's hard to get zucchini this time of year." She added, "Yobo, you go to the car and wait for me. I'll be right back." She took the crosswalk again to the other side of the street.

My father waited. He had time to study all the articles on display in the windows of the shops near his parked car. After a while he thought it seemed his wife was gone unduly long. Perhaps he should go to the Okada stand to see if she needed help.

He ignored a crowd of people gathered near the crosswalk. He had to walk around them. In passing, however, curiosity led him to what was attracting the people.

There was a woman lying on the ground. He reacted with sudden disbelief. The person injured on the ground was his wife! Her dress was pulled up, apparently from a fall. He quickly took off his shirt and covered her legs. Numbed and trembling, he addressed the police and told who he was.

An ambulance arrived. He accompanied his wife to Queen's Hospital. There he phoned his personal physician.

My brothers, sister, and I were called later to the hospital. Alarmed, not knowing what to expect, we met in the lobby and made our way to our mother. When we entered the room, we saw the doctor and a nurse administering a blood transfusion.

Our father's face was ashen. He was gripping the metal foot of the bed. His eyes were fastened on the bottle the nurse held in her hand.

Our mother looked serene. She did not look like someone in pain. Her eyes were closed and her lips wore a faint smile, as if she were enjoying a dream. I walked up to the side of the bed and, leaning over, I whispered, "How do you feel, Mama?" I waited for an answer while I held her hand. She did not respond.

After a long, long while the doctor declared that our mother was unconscious. We couldn't believe what he said next: "There's nothing more I can do to save your mother."

"What? Why?" we cried, stunned.

He did not say any more. We had the terrible feeling he had spoken all there was to say and done all that he could do.

Shaking with disbelief, we hovered closer to the figure lying on the bed. We prayed, sobbing and hoping for signs of life.

We waited a long time. Not until a nurse told us it was time to leave did we move. It was dark outside of the hospital.

It took days for the shock of our mother's death to sink in. The news of the fatal accident appeared on the front pages of the papers. When the suppliers of the tent and the foods were notified to cancel the orders, they replied they already knew of the circumstances and expressed their sympathy. "Tragic, so tragic," they all said. They expected no compensation, and some even offered to refund the deposits that had been made. It was much too sad a happening for a family to bear, they said, "a wedding turned into a funeral."

Many friends of the family came to the house on Rocky Hill to offer condolences. Cars lined the street for blocks on the three evenings prior to the funeral. The women who were closest to our mother took charge of the kitchen and prepared meals for the family and served refreshments to callers. A prayer service was conducted each evening by the Reverend Eiucho Chung. His wife, weeping, repeated over and over, "Your mother was so good. I can never forget how kind she was and how hard she tried to make my husband's and my life easier here at the parish." As she was a dressmaker, she insisted on sewing the dresses for my sister and me to wear to the funeral. White was traditionally worn for mourning. My father and brothers would wear white suits.

At first the anguished words, weeping, and sighs were all we heard from the callers. But those sounds gradually diminished and I became aware of the guests' whisperings and strange murmurings, which made me feel uneasy. The callers cast glances toward our father every now and then. What were they saying under their breath?

The night before the funeral, a few moments before the prayer service was to begin, a woman boldly walked up to my father. "Mr. Kwon, do you know that in Korea when a death in a family occurs before a wedding, it is taken as a sign, a warning? We think it means the marriage of your son is ill-fated. You should ask him not to marry this girl—"

The woman stopped when she saw the look of astonishment come over my father's face. His heavy eyes opened wide, then narrowed with anger. "How can you say that! My son's marriage is not your business."

I trembled with confusion. Could they be right? How superstitious these people are, I thought.

Later that night after everyone had left, my husband said

something that disturbed me even more. "I know you and your family are very upset now. But, in your grief, you should not forget about suing the driver of the truck—that fifteen-year-old kid."

I could not entertain the idea. "We can't. We can't now. How can you suggest such a thing? This is a time for mourning."

"But your mother has been killed! You shouldn't let the killer go free."

I never mentioned the matter to anyone in the family. In retrospect, many years later, I wondered: what was a fifteen-year-old doing with a huge truck? Why wasn't he careful when he came to a crosswalk in busy Chinatown? Those were the days when society was not lawsuit-conscious and there were not many lawyers practicing. Why did my father's insurance company neglect to file charges against the driver? The answer is ironic: the truck that ran down my mother was insured by the same company that carried our insurance.

The enforced blackout during the war had broken one time-honored Korean tradition—that of paying respect to the dead. From the moment the body was ready for viewing, it was the custom for family and close friends to gather together day and night before the funeral to observe a prolonged wake around the clock. But after December 1941, the all-night vigil was abandoned. Strangely, no one missed it, and everyone agreed it was a sensible change. Some people mentioned how disrespectful and tasteless it used to be when some of the "mourners" passed the night sitting in an adjoining room laughing and joking, playing cards, even gambling and drinking; their excuse was they could not sit frozen in grief hour after hour through the night.

Scores of my mother's friends and acquaintances came to view her body at Borthwick's Parlor during the morning wake on the day of the funeral. The custom of serving lunch to those who stopped by at noon was still followed. Others, sitting on the lanai, visited friends and acquaintances over a cup of coffee or tea.

Our family, wearing the traditional white, sat in front of the bier, the women in a row on one side, the men on the opposite side. We greeted each caller with brief remarks and expressed our thanks for their condolences. My sister and I became so choked with tears that all we could do that morning was shake hands and nod our heads.

About noon one by one our family members took turns leaving the parlor for some refreshments. When it was my turn, I went out to the lanai. I found the bowl of hot soup and rice gave me such a surge of renewed strength that I ate with relish. My teary, drooping eyes were opened. Just at that moment I caught sight of an old lady sittting nearby. She whispered to her neighbor, loud enough for me to hear, "Look at Hee Kyung's daughter. How can she enjoy eating at a time like this. She doesn't even look sad." I dropped my spoon, stood up, and left the table.

After the prayer service at the funeral parlor, we moved to the Korean Methodist Church on Keeaumoku Street for the formal funeral service.

The church and the lanai were filled to overflowing with friends. When the service of hymns and eulogies ended, the pallbearers carried the flower-draped casket down the center aisle— my mother was leaving her beloved church for the last time. Tears of sadness flowed from many eyes looking on. The hundreds of flower baskets banked in a wagon—gifts from mourners—followed the hearse. The monetary gift envelopes collected that day would be presented to the church.

The long procession of cars moved from the church up to Heulu Street and turned down on Kewalo. The hearse paused a long moment before the house where the wedding feast was to have been held, then proceeded to Diamond Head Memorial Park. There my mother, at age fifty-three, was laid to rest on June 26, 1947.

CHAPTER 18

The Korean Consulate

A QUIET settled over the family after we buried our mother. We were relieved of the strict rituals preceding a funeral and people hovering over us like honored guardians of the dead. We did not need to repeat the incidents leading to our mother's death to friends and acquaintances. But now we felt pure grief and despair, ours to bear alone.

The period was especially difficult for my father. He rose early each morning and drove to the gravesite, taking fresh flowers with him. For three months he made these trips to the memorial park. He remembered from his childhood his grand-father honoring his grandmother the same way after she had died.

One day a policeman stopped my father speeding on Ala Wai Boulevard. "What's the hurry? Where're you going?" the officer rebuked loudly as he pulled out his pad to write a ticket. "You were traveling over fifty-five miles an hour!"

When he received no reply, the officer looked up and noted the sad look on the driver. "By the way, where're you coming from?"

"From my wife's grave in Diamond Head." With his head down, he told of his predawn visits.

The officer folded his pad. He leaned over the door of the truck. "You must remember when you're on the road to drive carefully, within the speed limit." Then he turned and headed back to his motorcycle. He stopped and added, "You mustn't take your wife's death so hard. I'm sorry."

For my two brothers and my sister the future loomed dark

and fearful. They realized they had no one with whom "to talk over their plans in detail" as in the past. It was with their mother they had discussed their personal concerns; only the final decisions were usually conveyed to their father.

Young Chul decided to work at the pineapple cannery during the summer, and in the fall enter a mainland college to prepare for the ministry. My sister, Chung Hee, who was still in her teens, felt the weight of assuming the traditional duties of a woman of the household while she continued her schooling. For my older brother, Young Mahn, his immediate future was beset with problems. Aside from being torn between observing a respectful mourning period and the pleading of his fiancée to proceed with the wedding, he had his college degree to earn and a home to set up for his bride-to-be.

A month after his mother's funeral, Young Mahn was married. Sadly, because the mourning period was not over, no one from our family could bring ourselves to attend. But upon the insistence of my husband, we let our three-year-old daughter be flower girl.

I was busy with my own family—my husband and two little ones, yet memories of my mother filled my mind. I recalled the terrible times when she and I were separated and the special times when we were close. One August day we had sat together in the suffocatingly hot, curtained sedan chair on our way to Andong. Later, I had felt abandoned when she was imprisoned in Seoul for joining the radical movement in Korea to over-throw Japan's rule. By the time I was six years old I was sure I was to live permanently with my grandparents while my mother languished in a Yokohama prison. After we returned to Hono-lulu, how grateful I was to sit at her knee and learn English while all the children around me laughed at my Korean, the only language I knew. And how proud she was the day I gradu-ated from the university in cap and gown; we had our picture taken together on the campus. She wanted me to be married in style; and when my babies were born she insisted on keeping me confined in bed for a month while she fed me and my husband seaweed soup and chicken. She cleaned our house and did the laundry, too. I argued I had read in the papers that some women got up and even traveled on cruises with their husbands only two weeks after giving birth. But according to Korean beliefs I was not strong enough to emerge from bed until my baby was a month old.

Trade between the United States and Japan finally opened, and shipments of bamboo began arriving. My father immersed himself in the production of Poinciana Draperies again. The factory hummed with brisk postwar business. But grief, depression, and restlessness plagued him.

His grandchildren's visits to his Kakela home gave him some relief. Late in the afternoons I'd drive the children to be with him when he returned from work. He liked to lie sprawled on the long, comfortable chenille sofa near the windows overlooking the back lawn. One whole wall of the living room was windows; he could see across the houses and over rooftops as far as the University of Hawaii campus.

By chuckling and winking, he communicated well with Merphil, aged three, and Gary, two. He asked about their daily activities as if they were wondrous happenings. "Is that so!" he'd exclaim whether he understood their speech or not. They made him laugh.

Once he asked his granddaughter to bring him some toilet tissue. "Harabuji wants to read the paper," he explained, "and my glasses look dirty. I must clean them. Merphil, remember, I need only a *small* piece of paper."

She ran to the bathroom and quickly returned with a piece of tissue about one inch square.

"Ho, ho, ho. Grandpa cannot use this. Too small! Go get me some more paper."

The next thing he knew the little girl was dragging the whole roll of tissue to the living room.

Grandfather declared, "Eh, eh, eh—too much!" He jumped up and cried, "Ah, you! I should have gotten the paper myself." Then noticing the little girl's mouth twitching as if she were about to cry, he quickly added, "Ha, ha! Come. You and

Grandpa roll 'em up now." He mimicked a dancer and, laughing, together they rocked back and forth and rerolled the tissue to the bathroom.

His grandson liked to sidle up to him and chat. One day he asked, "What you drinking, Harabuji?"

"Oh, this is whiskey. You can't have this."

"Naw. That Coca Cola, I know. I want some."

"No, no, no, Gary. Grandpa put whiskey in Coke. You cannot have any of this."

An hour later I came in from the kitchen and found Gary laughing and giggling, trying to stand up, then falling, tumbling and rolling on the floor.

I was alarmed. "What's so funny?" I asked.

Grandpa was snoring on the sofa. Merphil, sitting on the carpet, flipping the pages of a magazine, said, "He's silly, Mommy."

"No. Something's wrong with your brother," I said. My son's face was flushed and his head feverish. He kept on giggling and falling. Then all of a sudden he ran to the bathroom. He threw up.

After I washed his face, he motioned he wished to lie down. As soon as he did, he fell asleep.

I walked back to the living room, wondering what had provoked his strange behavior. My eye fell on Grandpa's glass. I ran to it and found the ice had melted and the glass was empty.

A year passed. My father was still plagued with deep depression. Then one day he was struck by an idea; perhaps he could visit his favorite bamboo supplier, Miyoshi, in Osaka and ask about new lines of bamboo.

Then another idea struck him. He said to us, "Why don't I cross the sea from Japan and visit my brother? I haven't seen him for years." From their intermittent correspondence he knew that his brother Sang Kyu had a thriving opthalmology practice in Taegu. The hope of a reunion with his brother excited my father. Fortunately, travel in Korea was allowed by the newly formed Republic of Korea under President Syngman Rhee.

Before he left, my father asked me to help in the shop. He

begged, "Please oversee the operation while I'm gone." I was reluctant to go to work because my children were preschoolers. But I relented, provided I would put in only half a day.

The first letter I received from him told of the meetings with the Osaka bamboo weavers and the enthusiasm with which they had received him. The second letter reported his call on the Korean Consulate in Tokyo, where he applied for a visa to enter Korea. He was advised that a confirmation from President Rhee's immigration headquarters was required before the official stamp could be affixed on the passport. The process would take only a few days, he was told.

The letters from my father were short, the handwriting scrawly, almost illegible. The fragments of sentences written in English challenged me to read between the lines.

The third letter revealed his impatience. According to the consulate staff, my father's passport was being held up for some reason. Sang Kyu and his wife were already waiting in a hotel in Seoul, where they would meet my father.

What was holding up confirmation of his request to visit a brother? The statement issued at the consulate day after day was the same: "No official word received yet, Mr. Kwon."

Several weeks passed. My father's suspicions were roused. One day he asked point-blank why the Korean government would deny him entry into his homeland. The officious young men of the consulate exchanged sly glances. Then one of them said, "Mr. Kwon, which political party did you belong to in Hawaii?"

So that was the game being played. Although he could not see why it mattered now that Korea had won independence, he answered, "Dong Nip Dan."

The interrogator slapped his thigh and cried out in glee, "We thought so! We knew it! Your party opposed President Syngman Rhee and the Dong Ji Hoi!"

A feeling of indignation and helplessness swept over him. "You're telling me you won't let me in Korea because of my former political ties?"

The wily young men huddled together. They were all fair,

black-haired, and dressed alike in dark Western suits. None of them appeared taller than five-foot-six. They looked like schoolboys, whispering and casting conniving glances at their victim. Finally one of them broke away from the circle and, trying to conceal a smirking smile, announced, "There *is* a way we know you can get a visa, Mr. Kwon."

"What's that?"

The man took a few paces, paused, then swung around. "Mr. Kwon, we can help you if you give us . . . money."

How revolting, my father thought. A new Korean government was established and already there were signs of corruption. He did not wish to believe these men. He asked, "Can I wait for an official reply to my application?"

The answer came slowly: "You can if you have time to wait."

Back at the hotel my father pondered. Should he pass money under the table?

The principles of honesty and integrity, which had served him well all his life, prevailed. He made up his mind. He wired his brother, saying he could not procure a visa. Then he left the Orient.

When I heard why the much-anticipated reunion with his brother had not taken place, I was disappointed and rebuked my father. He replied by blasting the Korean officials he had encountered in Tokyo.

I argued, "Why should you let them spoil your plans? After all, your brother whom you haven't seen—"

"No!"

"For once in your life you could have compromised—"

"No. Never."

To everyone's astonishment sales of Poinciana Bamboo Draperies soared as the days went by. Meanwhile, the venetian blind dealers again were grumbling, contending they were losing much of the business which should be theirs to D. Kwon & Co. In fierce competition among themselves, the dealers engaged in slashing prices, deliberately lying about other dealers, and promising delivery of goods faster than anyone else.

Gradually they decided "if they couldn't fight 'em, join 'em." One by one of the venetian blind manufacturers humbly approached my father and requested a wholesale dealership. Offering a franchise was a new experience for my father. He had legal papers drawn up for each assignment of dealership and a one-time fee was required from each dealer for the right to represent Poinciana. The legal document clearly stipulated that the bamboo draperies were to be manufactured only in the D. Kwon factory.

The interior decorators in town were a competitive lot but they were not necessarily after the same customers. These decorators looked for original ways of using bamboo; they scoffed at the "common people" who covered nearly every window in their houses with the Kwon product. Some decorators haughtily claimed that Poinciana Draperies looked stiff in a room because the bamboo material folded in such relentlessly precise symmetry, whereas cloth draperies tended to hang loosely and give a soft look. Despite their criticisms and eccentricities they did create some beautiful blinds and draperies by combining the bamboo with rich damasks, varicolored cords, and fancy metal accessories.

CHAPTER 19

Mr. J

ONE day a haole businessman, a longtime customer and friend of my father, dropped in the shop. After exchanging greetings and general comments about "business in Hawaii noticeably picking up," Mr. J stepped into the factory. He observed the employees moving with skill and efficiency from task to task.

"Kwon, you got a good bunch of workers," he commented. "Yes, you got a good operation going." His voice sounded less than casual to my father. He wondered what he should anticipate or suspect of the visitor, who was an attractive man with curly brown hair, an engaging manner, and an appearance younger looking than his fifty years. Mr. J ran a very successful lumber business.

The two men walked through the factory, passed the cutters, seamstresses, traverse-track makers, and painters. My father often permitted his friends to go through his plant. The men stopped when they reached the carpenter shop, where Mr. J let his eye record the ample supply of wood neatly stacked on two floors.

Then they went outside to the driveway next to the factory. For a while there was no sound but the crunch of their steps on the gravel. The sun nearing the noon hour beat down on them.

Finally Mr. J spoke. "Kwon, I want to talk to you about something."

"Yeah? About what?"

"I—I've got a proposition to make. How would you like to form a corporation? I was thinking, you get 51 percent of the shares. Me and three others put up one hundred thousand dollars, but we get 49 percent of the vote."

My father was taken by utter surprise. A most unusual offer. "Who these other men?" he asked.

"They're my friends. I will introduce you to them, of course. They're all businessmen. We believe you have a good product and we think we can make Poinciana Draperies something really big. We *all* can make money, I believe."

Mr. *J* noticed my father pondering over what he had just said. He advised, "You take your time and think about it, Kwon. I'll talk to you again. Call me if you have any questions." Then they shook hands and parted.

That evening Father invited our family out to dinner. We knew that whenever he asked us to a restaurant, he wished to discuss his business. At the dinner were my husband, our two children, and me; also my sister, brother, and my brother's wife.

We heard the details of the proposal made by Mr. *J*. At first we were all pleased. The offer sounded very good. As the evening progressed, however, our reactions changed. We raised questions and expressed anxieties regarding the risks involved.

My sister and I were more inclined to favor the corporation move with the four businessmen friends, while my husband and my brother were apprehensive. "Why don't we keep the business in the family?" one of them suggested. At that moment Father beamed; apparently he liked that idea. "On the other hand," my brother said, "think how much easier it will be for you, Abuji, to have a big corporation launch the mainland market as you have been planning. We're such a small family. It might be hard for us to open a branch in a big city. Wouldn't it be easier to have money and shareholders backing us?"

The fear of the four investors possibly mismanaging the business disturbed my husband and my brother. One remarked, "If the corporation loses money, Abuji might lose his patent rights. Then what?"

Nothing was settled that evening. What we really needed was the astute advice of skilled attorneys, a notion that none of us had entertained.

D-Day, the day my father would render his decision to accept or reject the offer of Mr. J and his associates, was set for a Tuesday, at 2:00 P.M. Mr. J would come alone to the Kakela house.

The week preceding D-Day was fraught with unease and tension for our whole family. My father could not concentrate on work. He went on long drives or stayed at home and brooded. Several times he had met and talked with the interested investors. One morning he was willing to incorporate his business with them; the next morning he changed his mind.

When his cronies heard of the business deal being considered, their opinions sat evenly divided on opposite sides of the fence. One group declared, "It is an excellent chance to make Poinciana big. You could never really do it alone, Mr. Kwon." The opposing group warned of the danger in becoming involved with "haoles who could overpower you."

The morning of the fateful day my sister telephoned me. "I'm so nervous. Could you come and sit with me today?" she asked. When I got to the Kakela house my sister remarked, "Abuji looks good today. His face is clear. He's very cheerful."

"He is?" I was surprised. "What has he decided?"

"He hasn't decided one way or the other. He says if Mr. J does not show up today or if he's not here by two o'clock sharp, he's going to forget the deal."

"What?" I exclaimed. I couldn't believe what I heard. I shook my head. On the delicate element of Mr. J's showing up at the appointed time hinged the resolution of a most critical matter. It was like flipping a coin in the air to decide one's future.

While Father waited in the living room, my sister and I sat in a back bedroom. When Mr. J arrived, we would slip out into the hall and eavesdrop on the dramatic meeting.

Two o'clock came and went. Two-thirty. Three o'clock. Ten minutes after three o'clock a car roared up the hill and stopped abruptly in front of the house. The doorbell rang. Our father opened the door.

It was Mr. J. "I'm sorry I'm late, Kwon."

"It's too late!"

"I couldn't help it. We had a lot of things still to hash out at the last minute. I'll tell you about them." Mr. J sounded apologetic and tired, yet eager to talk.

"We agreed 2:00 P.M. Remember?" We thought our father's voice was cold and hard.

"Let's sit down, Kwon, and talk. What did you decide?"

My sister and I crept out of the bedroom and watched the two men walk toward the far wall of windows in the living room. They sat down. Abuji looked angry; his mouth was closed tight, his posture stiff. Then we heard him say with finality, "I got nothing to say to you. Don't speak to me. You come too late."

"Now, Mr. Kwon, you can't mean that—"

"Yes, I mean it. You don't know how much I think and worry about this. But I give you chance until two o'clock! I promise myself that."

"Well, now, Kwon," Mr. *J*'s tone was conciliatory and at the same time incredulous. "You can't mean the deal is off?"

There was a long, long silence. Mr. *J* fidgeted in his chair. Our father sat stiff and still.

Finally Mr. *J* rose from his chair, disappointment and defeat on his face. He raised his hand to his forehead and uttered, "My friends and I were willing to put up a lot of money—twenty-five thousand dollars each. We wanted to be sure we were doing the right thing. But I guess you were worried, too. Looks like your mind is made up." He walked slowly toward the front door, turned, and said, "I'm sorry it turned out this way, Kwon." He let himself out the door.

The next few days Father acted as if his life was clearly mapped. He reserved a seat on Pan American for San Francisco. He said he believed the branch shop for Poinciana Draperies should be located there instead of in Los Angeles.

And, to my surprise, he asked my husband to invest five thousand dollars and become a partner in the family business. To my astonishment, without hesitation, my husband pulled out of his family's liquor business and agreed to become one of the managers of the new partnership. He, like Mr. *J,* believed there was great promise in the Poinciana product.

Again we were invited by Father to dinner. To celebrate the recent turn of events, we went to the new Don the Beachcomber restaurant in Waikiki. Our family of eight was ushered into a tropical dining room with highly polished *ohia* wood tables in a setting of lush ferns and island flowers. The table tops were cut in graceful curves and two or three could be neatly joined, as was done for us, for added length and width. The smiling Hawaiian waiters, dressed in white and sashed in red, leisurely served the food in monkeypod bowls and plates. They moved gracefully, as if they were dancing. At the end of the meal I learned the bill came to the exorbitant amount of forty dollars —in those days the equivalent to a month's rent for an average family.

That evening Father was in a jaunty, expansive mood. He told us he would open the San Francisco shop just as soon as he could find a suitable location. He had friends in the Bay Area, including a Methodist pastor who once served in Honolulu.

He advised us he would put Young Mahn in charge of the branch established on the mainland. He urged Young Mahn, "You study hard. Take all the business courses you can so you will be a successful businessman."

We smiled as we watched Father enjoying his dinner and joking with the waiters. There was an endearing charm about him that drew people to him and they remembered him. Perhaps it was because of his childlike optimism and great relish for what lay in the future.

CHAPTER 20

In the Big City

WE went to Honolulu airport to see our father off to San Francisco. He was leaving our small town of barely five hundred thousand people for a metropolis of millions. At age sixty-one, when most men were looking forward to retirement, here was a man bounding up the ramp of the Pan American plane—destined for a new business venture. He wore a new black wool suit on that warm June morning; he had heard that San Franciscans wear wool all year round. I did not ask my brother nor my sister how they felt, but I was worried. Would he be able to communicate in his pidgin English with people in a sophisticated city?

We heard nothing from him for a while. When he finally called it was to inform us he had leased a factory and office space in "a perfect location" in downtown San Francisco. He wished to open the shop immediately. I wondered that if Young Mahn could not be there until he graduated from college in a year, did my father plan to manage the branch himself?

When he returned we noticed our father was riding the crest of exuberance. He made announcements and issued statements that surprised us. First, he had decided to send me and my husband, with our children, to take charge of the new branch. "There is no time to waste," he said. "I already rented an apartment for you on Pacific Avenue."

I protested. Why should my husband and I with our two little ones be uprooted? How could we inaugurate the new business in a strange city on such short notice?

Then followed a speech on filial piety, the first of many on the subject I was to hear. "How can you say that? This is *our* family business, a business for all of us. We should all work together. You mother helped build it. Now it is your duty and your brothers' and sister's."

I had always respected and honored my parents' wishes and expectations in the past. But I thought we should have held a family discussion before such major decisions were made. Never before had I felt obligated to do something that appeared so difficult and demanding.

In the meantime, there were two very important matters for my father to attend to. One was the observance of the second anniversary of my mother's death. We visited the gravesite with flowers, and in the evening held a prayer service at the Kakela house. Besides the family, close friends were present. Several of the guests were widows. Unlike the previous year's observance when the mood was somber, this year's turned out to be quite different. Laughter, gaiety, games, and merriment were the order following the prayers. The women without spouses openly sought our father's favor. They extended invitations to him to attend dinners at their homes in his honor. Whether he was aware of being chased by husband-seekers we could not tell, but he was obviously enjoying his new popularity. It appeared to me that after his wife was dead two years, a man could take another mate.

The second important matter was placing a sizeable order of split bamboo to stock both the home and the branch shops. To import goods from Japan required a letter of credit from a bank. I accompanied my father to the Bank of Hawaii to procure this credit.

The officer at the bank noticed the inordinately large order. He remarked, "Mr. Kwon, this is way over your usual purchase budget, isn't it? You're asking us to guarantee a fifteen thousand dollar shipment?"

"Yes," my father replied proudly. "This is first time I order over million square of bamboo!"

"Hmm," the banker muttered, adjusting his glasses. "I must ask you how you plan to come up with the cash?"

"Oh, I have money. You no worry," was the quick reply.

Riffling through some papers, the banker noted, "Your business checking balance normally shows between two and four thousand dollars."

Trying to conceal his annoyance my father assured the officer, "I get my personal account."

"I'll have to ask you for a deposit this time. Eight thousand dollars. Did you say you can get this from another account of yours?"

"Yes. From bank across the street. You let me know when you want money."

By late July, 1948, my husband Philip and I were packed and ready to make the move to the West Coast with our children. We were starting a new life in new surroundings. We trembled at the thought of not knowing what to expect.

Unbelievably cool weather greeted us the evening we arrived in San Francisco. We had never before experienced chilling winds, biting and assaulting, in the middle of summer. When we stepped into the Pacific Avenue apartment, the greater chill in the rooms nearly drove us back to the street. The landlord, who lived above our apartment, was to have turned on the heat for us. Yet the heating system in the apartment, we learned soon enough, was old and faulty. We huddled close together and examined the rooms. An unpleasant odor permeated the place. (Later I got used to that odd smell of stagnant air trapped inside.) In the kitchen the smell was worse. We pushed open a window for relief but closed it immediately, for the outside air felt like ice particles blowing in.

Somehow we passed that first night.

The next morning we went to the garage below the apartment and found the station wagon my father had purchased for both company and personal use. For the first time I saw row houses up and down the hill, each attached to the next. These stuck-together dwellings disconcerted me. I wondered, didn't the people living in them feel boxed in?

We drove down Pacific Avenue, turned onto Powell, and

drove carefully over the cable car tracks, crossed the very broad Market Street, and were on our way to our factory on Sixth Street.

I was impressed with the city that morning. We had passed immaculate, smart-looking shops and hotels. There were only a few people who were already out on the clean streets. After we crossed Market Street, I noticed the shop fronts growing shabbier and shabbier looking. When we stopped at the entrance of what I presumed was our own place of business, I looked at Philip in dismay.

"This is it," he said. He had made a trip earlier to San Francisco.

"You mean this is the factory? Where is the office, and the showroom?"

He pointed to the shop with the small drab windows and one small door. "It's all there."

I suddenly felt overcome with disenchantment. I struggled to get out of the car. How could Father have done a thing like this? Where were his senses when he leased this place? Would any fashionably dressed San Franciscans think of coming down here to buy something beautiful for their homes? I could see derelicts nearby at the corner of Sixth and Mission streets, sharing a bottle of wine.

Our children scrambled out of the car. Their bodies leaning forward with excitement, they followed their father into the shop. They ran from room to room, up the wooden stairs into a small bedroom and a kitchenette, came down the same stairs and turned into a huge, high-ceilinged workroom. At the far end of this workroom hung a curtain on a circular clothes wire, suspended from the ceiling; the curtain could be drawn around the painter when he started his machine. All the windows were closed, yet it was freezing cold in the building.

A few minutes later our son came running toward us, his eyes bulging with alarm. "Mommy, Daddy," he cried, "there's a dead man outside!"

"Where?"

"Right outside the front door!"

"How do you know he's dead?" I asked as we all hurried to the entrance.

When Philip opened the door, we saw an old, unshaven man in a dirty, worn coat and tattered trousers, lying at our door-step. He lay rolled on his side in a fetal position. Was he dead? No one could enter or leave our shop without having to jump over him.

"What should we do?" I asked Philip. "Should we call the police or an ambulance?"

We heard some people passing by, mumbling as they circumvented the creature on the sidewalk, "These winos! These good-for-nothing bums."

When an onlooker noticed my stricken expression he said, "Don't worry, lady. The paddy wagon will be by soon to pick 'im up. They always cruise around here for punks like him." The man pointed derisively at the unmoving figure.

Sure enough. Before long a police wagon came by.

Before school started in September I shopped for warm clothes for the children. Like other shoppers in town, I walked fast; the crisp air made everyone appear full of resolute purpose. I saw crowds on the wide sidewalk fronting the stores. Inside, every store was bursting with customers. So this was a big city! I had never seen so many shoppers packed in shops. Busy elevators were monitored by snappily uniformed women, who made sure none of the cars was overfilled or left the floor without enough riders.

All of a sudden I was aware of the sea of *white* faces all around me. I could pick out only one or two women with yellow skin. And for the first time in my life I experienced prejudice. A sharp pain accompanied this strange feeling. With my Oriental face I found it difficult to flag a salesgirl. I was passed over time and time again. When there were three or four of us at a counter with articles to purchase, it was as if I were invisible. When I did finally get the attention of one salesperson, her voice seemed needlessly curt.

That day the only store where I forgot about prejudice was at

I. Magnin. There the merchandise was higher priced. But I found that the tall, elegant salesgirls, who looked like fashion models, seemed too busy to be choosing whom to favor. I saw Indian women in graceful saris leisurely strolling about, and richly gowned Chinese matrons, bejeweled with jade, being waited on. A few pigtailed Japanese girls flitted about examining the merchandise.

The bamboo stock arrived from Honolulu, and we made arrangements with a trucking firm for its delivery from the harbor to the shop. All was soon in readiness for what we hoped would be a rush of business. So absorbed had we been trying to set up the business, we had overlooked the means of attracting customers in the Bay Area.

I had brought photographs of the Poinciana Draperies and copies of ads that we had run. I called a paper; when the man from the *San Francisco Chronicle* came in response to my call, he did not say much. His disdainful glances around the premises and the sort of questions he asked indicated that he usually dealt with professional advertising agents.

"We're new here in San Francisco." I regretted my remark as soon as I made it. It was obvious we were a new firm. I went on, "To introduce our product, I thought we might run this ad."

He looked at the sample ad. He kept a poker face. The ad had worked well for us in Honolulu, but he probably thought it was amateurish; I had laid it out myself.

"You want to run it just as it appears here?"

Now, what did he mean by that statement? I wanted to say, "Why not?" Instead, I replied, "Yes. How much will it cost?"

I almost fainted when he quoted the price. I bit my lower lip. I should have expected things to cost more in a big city.

"Do you have the cut for this trademark?" he asked.

"Oh, no. We did not bring it. I should have remembered to—"

"Then, I guess, we'll have to make one ourselves." The man jotted down some notes next to the copy in his hand.

I thought perhaps it would be wise to order a smaller ad.

"For starters, could we run a two-column or maybe a three-column ad?" I asked.

"As you wish." The ad man sounded bored.

The first Poinciana advertisement brought us a deluge of calls —all from people who wished to *sell us* something: the latest electric typewriters, adding machines, fancy stationery, file cabinets, executive furniture. For several weeks salesmen presented smooth memorized spiels that wore me down. These men popped in and out of the shop. Calls from potential customers —none.

There was, however, one young salesman who impressed me with his low-key approach. He had brilliant blue eyes in a narrow, handsome face. The blue of his eyes contrasting with his dark hair and alabaster skin arrested my attention. He was slight of build and extremely polite, reminding me of the well-bred gentlemen in old English novels.

Norton Jacobs showed genuine interest in our Poinciana line, asking how they worked, how long they'd last, where the material came from, and what colors were available. Gradually he revealed he was a freelance advertising agent, and he had suggestions for our ads. Within a month we decided to retain him. Philip and I became good friends with Norton. He invited us to dinner to meet his mother in her apartment. She was a widow whose main interests seemed to be bridge and shopping.

The first of Jacobs' ads attracted possible customers but did not net us any sales. I saw cars driving past our shop on Sixth Street with well-dressed passengers peering into our store, then moving on. I wondered how many drunks were standing outside and whether they were scaring away the potential customers.

A former Honoluluan, who was familiar with our draperies, called to tell us how happy he was to know we were in San Francisco. In fact, he was our first customer. He lived in Bakersfield. He gave us our initial taste of success as well as our first experience in driving long distances to homes outside of San Francisco, where most of our future business lay.

Philip did not mind being taken as order-taker and measurer and installer of the draperies on these trips, and at the shop as foreman, inventoryman, and jack-of-all-trades. He even took over the sewing sometimes.

Repetition is an important key to successful advertising. Costly as it was, there was no alternative. When the first few curious customers set foot in our tiny showroom, there was reason to celebrate. I phoned Jacobs and told him the ads had triumphed.

I watched the would-be customers who braved their way into our shop. I noted that as soon as they opened the door and saw *me* they seemed apologetic and wanted to back out and leave. Once inside, they quickly viewed the displays, asked a few questions, then left.

I said to my husband, "I believe we need a *haole* front. Anyone who responds to our ad just seems to freeze and lose interest when they see an Oriental in this showroom."

So we hired an attractive young girl with golden hair framing her face, a peaches-and-cream complexion, and a pretty smile. It was amazing how quickly the drop-in trade improved. The blond Miss Shelley greeted customers with a most disarming smile. She spoke to them with ease, and oohed and aahed with them over the beauty of Poinciana.

My husband and I remained in the background. When he drove out to clients' homes to verify orders, he was taken as a factory hand skilled in his craft, not as the boss. I was merely the bookkeeper operating in the background.

By Thanksgiving Day—four months after our arrival—our factory was humming. We had gained a small foothold in the San Francisco economy.

At Christmas the city of San Francisco glowed with lights, brilliant ornaments, music-filled shops, and fresh-cut flowers at street corners. For the first time I found Christmas shopping tireless and enjoyable—the weather was invigorating.

Philip and I rejoiced that we had pre-holiday orders for Poinciana. On Christmas Eve we held a festive party at the shop for the employees.

At home the fake chimney in the living room added a measure of excitement for the children as they hung their long, red stockings and placed candles on the mantel. On Christmas night we accompanied our Korean landlord and his wife to their Methodist church for the Yule program. A thin, wiry Santa wearing the traditional red and white suit distributed toys and candy. I explained to Gary, the younger of our children, who still was thrilled with the notion of Santa, that a helper was sent because Santa himself was resting at the North Pole after the strenuous night before spent traveling all over the world.

We had a surprise visit from my brother, Young Mahn, who came the week after Christmas. He announced he was graduating the next month, in January, a semester earlier than expected because the University gave all veterans full credit for the December and January they had lost when Japan attacked Pearl Harbor.

"That's wonderful! You must be happy!" I congratulated my brother.

He met the workers and studied the operation of the factory. Young Mahn informed us he would be glad to take over the San Francisco branch in two or three months.

That meant Philip and I would be relieved of our post. Our children could go barefoot again, swim, and picnic in the Hawaiian sun.

At first Philip resisted the thought of leaving. He had put in countless hours of hard work to make the San Francisco branch a viable business. I could see he was attached to the few workers who had shared with him the vision of success. But because I wanted so much to leave the cold, big city for home, he relented. Besides, he missed his mother's very special kim chee, that hot, red-peppered cabbage that caused one's ears to ring. I knew, too, that he looked forward to wearing casual clothes again instead of the coat and the constricting necktie.

In January, 1950, the coldest temperature in fifty years hit the Bay Area. At noon one day it was thirty-five degrees when I stood outside the grocery store on Pacific Avenue near our home with a wool cap and my coat up to my ears. I watched with disbelief a round-faced man from China. He was wearing no jacket, no shirt, only his pants and a pair of gloves, and carrying a side of frozen beef from his wagon on the street to his freezer.

"Hey, aren't you cold?" I hollered out to him.

"This nicee," he chuckled, grinning and slapping his chest. "I likee!"

When it rained, driving up and down the steep hilly roads and over cable car tracks became extremely hazardous. I couldn't wait to leave San Francisco.

Spring arrived. Young Mahn and his wife Grace, with their infant daughter, were ready to move into our apartment.

By that time Philip and I were packed and ready for the post back in Honolulu.

CHAPTER 21

Losing the Gamble

THE decade of the 1950s began with everything looking rosy for my father. He felt assured that the business he had built would remain in the family, with his eldest son Young Mahn secure in the San Francisco office, and my husband Philip and me in charge of the home office. He hoped his daughter Chung Hee would join the firm when she graduated from college. From his other son, Young Chul, who was committed to the ministry, he could expect no help.

But as the wheels of life move and shift, so do the postures and poses of people. My husband, hearing of the education benefits in the GI Bill of Rights for Veterans, decided to enroll at Baylor University in Texas to get his degree. As a part of a family who revered a college degree so highly, he did not wish to pass up the opportunity to finish the two years more of schooling he needed for that degree.

And Chung Hee said she planned to continue her education in New York after graduation in June. How proud our father was the day she walked up in cap and gown on the Manoa campus to receive her diploma. Unable to hold back his tears, he sighed, "How much greater our joy would be today if your mother were with us!"

A week later Father left on another of his frequent trips to the mainland to check the progress of the San Francisco operation. Not three days after his arrival there, he was struck down in a crosswalk on Sixth Street by a marine in a ramshackle car purchased a few hours earlier. The marine, who was on shore leave at the time, had no insurance.

Young Mahn called me to report the accident. He said our father had suffered a skull fracture and at the moment was unconscious. I immediately contacted my sister who happened to be at a graduation party. She hurried home, threw a few things together in a suitcase, and flew out on the next plane.

She went straight to the hospital, where she found our father in a coma. For days she sat next to his bed in the hospital, hoping he would open his eyes and acknowledge her presence.

On the day of the accident, she learned, an operation was performed for the injury sustained to the brain. During the operation the doctors discovered an old tumor, probably the result of a previous injury. But because so much blood had been lost, the doctors reserved removing the tumor until a later date. My sister's brief messages to me by phone were terribly depressing. She implied she spent each day praying for his recovery, not daring to think or look ahead to anything else.

After two weeks, by some miracle, her prayers were answered. Incoherent sounds emerged from our father's lips and his eyes gradually opened. The doctors were pleased, although they discovered half of their patient's body was paralyzed and no sense could be made of the sounds he uttered. But day by day he improved, growing clearer-eyed and stronger. Only his limbs and speech remained impaired.

After several conversations on the phone, we decided our father should come home to Honolulu for the second operation. It was to be performed by Dr. Ralph B. Cloward, the leading brain surgeon in Hawaii. The San Francisco doctors approved.

In those days Pan American provided two berths in the rear of the plane, one on each side of the aisle. Father occupied one, and my sister the other. He was moved by ambulance from hospital to plane; then in Honolulu, by ambulance from plane to another hospital.

The young, brilliant Dr. Cloward held witty one-way dialogues with his patient. He knew by the patient's eyes that the jokes and thoughts being expressed were understood. After the operation to remove the old tumor in the brain, Dr. Cloward noted that our father still could not raise his left arm, and his speech consisted of mere grunts and sighs. The doctor jested about his patient's irresponsible plumbing.

One morning I happened to be visiting at the hospital when Dr. Cloward came in looking especially cheery. He began, "How's the water works this morning, Mr. Kwon?" The patient replied with an annoyed hiss.

Then the doctor brusquely ordered: "Mr. Kwon, raise your left arm as high as you can!" My father made a vain attempt as he had done many times in the past weeks without success.

The doctor then stalked up to the side of the bed and he deliberately yanked my father's arm straight up in the air. There was a sharp crack. The next sound was louder: "God damn you, son of a bitch!" My father lay gasping and moaning in pain. He had uttered his first comprehensible words since his accident.

After a few days he was permitted to go home to recuperate, with nurses attending him around the clock. He found it pleasanter and more comfortable at home. The nurses exercised his leg and arm continually. His speech was still garbled.

Friends began stopping by to visit at the Kakela house. They spoke cheerfully when they sat in our father's room, but when they came out their faces were long. They shook their heads and made depressing remarks to my sister and me: "Your father is not well. He seems all right, but he makes such weird sounds. We don't understand him at all"; "He will never be normal again. Too bad, his wonderful brain is permanently damaged"; "He tries so hard to talk but we can't make out what he's saying. He was such a fine man once . . ."

The visitors invariably left us feeling low for a few days. Would he ever speak coherently again? Somehow hope always stayed with us. We did not doubt that complete recovery was possible. The only question in our minds was how long would it take? We did not know of stories about people with brain damage who "became vegetables" and were institutionalized.

Day after day my sister and I took turns, patiently helping our father to his feet and urging him to take a few steps at a time. We bought a cane for him. Then we taught him to talk, beginning by asking him to label aloud the objects in the room. He was like a little child learning his first words. He practiced his speech lessons diligently. We noted that the better coordinated he became with his hands and feet, the more coherent became his speech.

There were good days when he was up and about from bedroom to living room, and there came days when he regressed and remained in bed. The secret to a continuing recovery, we soon learned, was not to force or to rush it.

One day he surprised us with the question: "How's the business in San Francisco?"

My sister and I pretended we were busy and did not hear him. We did everything we could to avoid answering him.

Young Mahn had written some months before, "Business here is tough. I need money badly to pay the bills." We sent him funds to cover his debts, calling them "loans from the home office."

Exactly one year after the accident, our father was able to make his first trip down to the shop. The daily visits were brief and disturbing. Slowly he perceived that we had been sending thousands of dollars to keep the San Francisco business afloat. He did not approve our action.

"Stop sending money to your brother!" he advised. "Let me take care of it." He withdrew from his personal account month after month. He knew he could not make the journey to the other shop. One day he asked my sister to make the trip and report to him "what exactly is the matter up there."

Chung Hee's reports via telephone were clear but discouraging. "The shop is busy," she said, "but Young Mahn keeps losing money." One day she called to say, "He wants to move the business site to a better location, to Howard Street, a few blocks away from here. And he thinks he should go in the cloth drapery business, too. Two men, who are drapery experts, want to work for him. In fact, they would like to go into partnership with him."

To all these requests, my father acquiesced. If that was the kind of boost the Poinciana business needed to survive, well,

"Let's see what he can do when I send him more money." He sold his large-income property on Prospect Street, consisting of five rental units, to give the West Coast branch the financial shot it needed.

With the last of the nurses discharged and my sister gone from the Kakela house, I was concerned about my father being alone when he went home after work. I need not have worried, for some of his friends had thoughtfully arranged for Mrs. Chun, a Korean widow, to serve as housekeeper, cook, and day nurse. She was not a member of the Korean Methodist Church.

Interestingly, during this interlude, a romance developed between Mrs. Chun and my father. He was still weak; the gloom of the faltering business in San Francisco no doubt slowed his recovery. But Mrs. Chun proved a real help. She prepared nutritious meals of seaweed soup and vegetable broths, and tasty meat, chicken, and fish dishes.

Soon my father could drive, at first for short trips, then for longer rides out to the country with Mrs. Chun.

One afternoon I happened to stop at the Kakela house to consult my father about some urgent matter. He was napping in his room, and Mrs. Chun was reading on the long, yellow sofa in the living room. I had rushed in from the hectic business world, and here was soft-spoken Mrs. Chun relaxing in the cool, restful house.

I decided to wait awhile until my father woke up. I fell into a big chair near the sofa.

Mrs. Chun glanced at me timidly. She had a plain, square face without much color. Only her gentle smile was what one remembered about her.

I thought I should say something appropriate. "Mrs. Chun, I appreciate what you're doing for my father."

"That's all right," she said, paused a moment, then added, "You know, your father wants me to marry him."

I was jolted. "Is that so—?" I stammered, trying to suppress my astonishment.

"Didn't he tell you?"

"No—not yet."

She showed me the large diamond on her left hand. I blinked. "That's very nice," I said softly.

None of us children had heard from our father of his impending marriage to Mrs. Chun. We knew he had what Koreans call "heavy lips"; that is, "lips that do not divulge secrets nor indulge in idle gossip." But why was he withholding his intention to marry her?

As my father spent more hours each day at the shop, he seemed to need Mrs. Chun less and less. She still went up to his house and gave it a daily cleaning as well as cooked his dinner; then she left.

I waited for some word relating to the wedding date, but none came.

I overheard one day at church that some of the church ladies and their husbands were socializing at the Kakela house almost every evening "so that he wouldn't be lonely." They chatted and played games, particularly the popular game called *yute,* in which the players threw various-shaped pieces of wood on a board punctured with holes. They played the game for hours, shouting and laughing, rejoicing boisterously when they won, feigning anger and frustration when they lost. Mrs. Chun was excluded from these soirees.

Several months passed. I wondered about the status of Father's romance with the lady to whom he had given the large diamond. One day I bumped into a Mrs. Kim in town. She was one of the ladies who frequented the soirees. Out of curiosity I asked her, "Did you hear that my father's getting married soon?"

She looked momentarily shocked. "Who said that?"

"Well, Mrs. Kim, isn't that true?"

"You mean to—to Mrs. Chun?"

"Yes."

"No, I doubt that very much." She shook her head. "How can your father think of marrying a woman like that? Your mother was such a good woman. This Mrs. Chun—is different."

"Different?"

"Chung Sook, no decent woman would stay in a man's house with him day and night—alone with him."

"But that was when she was a nurse to him!" I defended her.

"But that doesn't look good from the outside. Like low-class people might do that. Your father can find somebody better for a wife."

So these Methodist women would instill guilt and deny my father the woman he cared for because of some mythical "goodness" that Mrs. Chun lacked. I understood finally why she faded from her betrothed's life.

The news from San Francisco continued to be gloomy and bleak. Young Mahn admitted that despite the infusion of so much money, the business still was failing.

For a long while his wife, Grace, was seriously ill and required hospitalization intermittently. Her mother went up to help care for the little daughter. Grace continued to need intense medical care and long hospitalization. No wonder Young Mahn could not give the attention the business required with his wife so ill.

When my father was compelled to sell his Kakela residence to raise more money for the failing branch, he vowed it would be the last piece of property he would sacrifice to finance his mainland venture.

Two years later the San Francisco shop was permanently closed. According to my father's calculations he lost $150,000 in his gamble to establish a Poinciana Draperies branch on the West Coast.

Young Mahn decided to remain on the mainland with his family and look for employment there, and Chung Hee returned home to work in the Honolulu shop.

My husband returned home about this time after finishing his studies at Baylor and receiving his degree. He informed me that Johns Hopkins University was holding a place for him in the fall. He wondered whether he was too old to study for a medical career, but he knew many veterans in their late thirties, like him, were preparing for professional jobs requiring graduate work.

After much pondering, however, Philip believed it was really not fair for him to leave me and the children again. We had been separated by the war and by the years he had been away at Baylor. He made up his mind to join his brother in a new, promising charter-boat business.

For a spell, a period of peace reigned over our family. Some of the old men at the Methodist church persuaded my father to forget his problems and study with them to become U.S. citizens. His cronies spoke enthusiastically about their naturalization classes and how they enjoyed helping each other with the lessons. After months of diligent studying, each of them succeeded and was formally granted U.S. citizenship. How proud and happy they were to become American citizens!

The crowning cap to this period took the form of a happy seventieth birthday celebration for our father at the beautiful Lau Yee Chai restaurant. A hundred friends and associates honored him at a sumptuous Chinese banquet given by his children; a tenth course was added to the menu at the last moment because "fried noodles presaged good health and long life."

Before the decade of the 1950s ended, the wheels of life turned dramatically, bringing to our family an unprecedented series of crises and griefs.

A bold fellow, *LS,* suddenly appeared on the business scene in Honolulu and infringed on my father's bamboo drapery patent. He began selling cheap imitations of Poinciana, calling them "tropical blinds and drapes." His store also carried a variety of rattan and bamboo furniture imported from the Philippines and Hong Kong. *LS,* a recent arrival from California, spread the word that the blinds he sold were rampant along the West Coast, especially in Los Angeles. He was sharp and clever, determined to stay in the Honolulu market.

My father was shocked. All the venetian blinds dealers in

town watched the scenario unfolding with keen interest. Would Mr. Kwon drag the infringer to the courts? After years of enjoying exclusive rights to his invention, what would Mr. Kwon do?

Our attorney, Herbert Choy, sent letters and warnings to *LS*. All the letters were refused and returned unopened. In the next weeks and months, correspondence between the U.S. Patent Office attorneys and Herbert Choy brought little relief to the situation. The attorneys said they needed time to scrutinize the patent. Time passed. In the meantime, the cheap, unpainted, unhemmed drapes sold by *LS* were bought by customers who did not care about quality. This cheaper product slowly flooded the market.

LS's blatant exploitation of my father's patent was slowly chipping away the strength and courage and resourcefulness my father once had. His head injury took its toll, and all of a sudden everything seemed too much for him to handle. He was embittered over the San Francisco failure. His lawyers' ineffectiveness roiled him. He could not provoke the action he desired from anyone. He, who once found so much humor and fantasy in life, turned irritable, sour, and difficult. Worst of all, in his eyes my sister and I did nothing right; we were always at fault.

In 1959 my sister left for Colorado with her husband, who went to study for a law degree. They took their little daughter with them. Chung Hee had found her means of escape from Father's wrath.

I tried to escape, too. I had a job offer from Sanford Weintraub in the advertising department of a local paper. When I told my father of my decision to work elsewhere, he broke down and cried, "How can you leave this business? I built this business for you and your brothers and sister. You can draw any amount of money you want. Don't leave. Don't leave me."

No matter how much I tried to reason with him that my decision was best for all concerned, he would not agree.

I relented and decided to stay with him.

Then a tragedy befell me and my children. My husband suddenly passed away in his sleep. I knew the members of his family had a history of high blood pressure and that each member took medication regularly for that condition. To everyone's surprise, although he was the youngest in the family and the one who looked the healthiest, he suffered a heart attack. Neither the children nor I had anticipated it, nor understood why he was taken from us. It was a sad day when we buried him at the National Cemetary of the Pacific in Punchbowl Crater.

A few months later I found it imperative to preserve my dignity and sanity by engaging in some other kind of work. Father was impossible to please. He lived alone and was too proud to admit defeat or that he needed help. He let out his frustrations by yelling and criticizing everyone he came in contact with. And he stringently controlled the company's purse strings. He chided me again and again for his children's faults, "the foolish spending of his money on fancy ideas for running a business." "Look what happened," he cried bitterly.

My plans to leave the family business had to be secret. I should not alarm him. I stole away in the mornings to attend classes at the University of Hawaii and returned in the afternoon to work at the shop.

There was a shortage of secondary teachers in Hawaii, I knew, and in order to fill vacancies the State Department of Education offered an accelerated eighteen-month Professioanl Certificate Program to applicants with a B.A. degree. I registered for this program in the fall of 1959. I attended classes in the morning only, and in the afternoon I returned to work in the shop.

To my amazement the D. Kwon & Co. business rolled along as though it were an engine set on wheels to run automatically. The honest and efficient crew we had working in the factory completed orders procured by the sole salesman on the staff. Since the company operations moved smoothly month after month, my father did not suspect the reason for my absence half of each day.

CHAPTER 22

Up in Smoke

THERE did come the time when my father learned I was preparing to leave the company and become a teacher. That information reached him indirectly one day and it must have caused much unexpressed resentment. He reacted by suddenly refusing invitations to have dinner with me and the children. And although he had the apartment next door to us he hardly paid any attention to his grandchildren, whom he loved dearly.

I approached him again and again, and persisted in pressing him to eat home-cooked meals with us. Finally he relented and agreed on one condition: that he pay for the groceries and for the services of a cook.

So I hired a Mrs. Pang. She was a big, strong woman with greying hair. Her unusually large, rolling eyes gave her the appearance of a person who had many ideas and opinions but rarely had a chance to express them. She made a familiar picture every afternoon walking up Kewalo Street to our apartment, carrying a floral parasol in the sun to protect her dark complexion.

Mrs. Pang took an immediate liking to my father. Not only did she respect him as her boss, but there was something about him that commanded her respect. She tried hard to please him. "Mr. Kwon, I hope—" she started haltingly one day, "I hope you like my cooking." And he replied, "Yes, yes, thank you."

One of Mrs. Pang's specialties and one of my father's favorites was a gelatin dessert—incredibly smooth, clear, softly firm, and delicious. She made it almost everyday. She set the table, cleared the sink, and left dinner warming in the oven or cooling in the refrigerator before she left.

After two years the services of Mrs. Pang abruptly ended when a fire broke through our two-story apartment building. On that windy night the fire raged mercilessly through the apartments, damaging them beyond repair. The tenants lost everything they owned. One lady said she did not care about her possessions but she mourned the death of her parakeet; she said she and her husband had been out and returned too late to save the bird.

According to the Chief's report there was good evidence that the fire started from a burning cigarette lodged between the cushions of an upholstered sofa in a studio rented by a university professor. He had entertained a guest that evening before driving her to the airport.

As did all the tenants, I lost every piece of my clothing. I was given a week to replenish my wardrobe before meeting my students again at the University Lab School where I was practice-teaching.

Finding other living quarters for my father and my family did not take long, but I was very sorry we became separated when he took only a room near the shop.

How many more crises could my father endure? He was facing ruin all around him. His attorneys had lost the momentum to take to court the parties who encroached on his patent. Perhaps if my father himself had pursued the case more vigorously, or perhaps if other members of the family cooperated with him in the fight, the violators would have been prosecuted. But, sadly, the family's interests and concerns were scattered.

After the fire, the black, ugly hulk of the Kewalo apartment building looked like it had been ripped by bombs. It stood unattended for weeks. The plumbing and electrical lines were severed, leaving the place untenantable, yet the insurance claims adjustor went about measuring what was still standing of the building and estimated the remains as "recoverable" from the claim.

"How can I use any part of this building?" my father argued. "Can't you see I'll have to rebuild completely before anyone can live in it?"

"I'm sorry," the adjustor said wryly, "it would have been better if the building had burned down to the ground. Then you could have claimed the full amount of your insurance."

The nearby residents complained that the sight of the torn up, sooty building was repulsive. Moreover, they said, the smells of charred wood, dead rats, and rotting foods in the damaged refrigerators pervaded the neighborhood.

I was caught in the throes of exams and completing my intern teaching, besides doing bookkeeping at the shop. I regretted I could not find a fraction of an hour to rebut the insurance man nor to attend to the neighbors' complaints.

Finally my father wired my sister to return from Colorado and help him clean up after the fire. Whatever the claims adjustor offered was accepted. The damaged building was demolished and the space it had occupied was cleared and sanitized.

Early in 1962 my father's health began failing rapidly and he made frequent trips to the doctor. According to the tests administered, his doctor said, gallstones were the cause of his suffering. The operation to remove the stones ended successfully, but the recovery was exceedingly slow.

Father lay in the hospital bed, a small, frail-looking man in white bedclothes, hardly moving or speaking. He had lost much weight. The doctor assured me there was no reason why Father should not be well soon—"he has not one germ in his body now." One day in a weak voice Father managed to make a request: he wished to see all his children.

My brother Young Mahn was summoned from the mainland. Young Chul was serving as a minister in a church in Hawaii. My sister Chung Hee and her family had returned home from Colorado. Surrounded by his children, or with one of us sitting at his side each hour of the day and evening, our father was comforted. We knew that the business he loved so much was on his mind but he had neither the strength nor the words to ask about it. He had fought and triumphed over innumerable adversities during his lifetime. We wondered, could he win once more?

Before dawn, on April 24, 1962, at the age of seventy-three, our father died in his sleep. The illness had been so brief that many of his friends at the church were surprised by the news of his death. He was buried next to our mother at the Diamond Head Memorial Park.

What to do with the business posed a serious problem for my brothers, sister, and me. Should the loyal D. Kwon & Co. employees be allowed to continue working in the factory as they were doing with no family member actively involved as administrator? We agreed that would be an odd arrangement.

We talked and talked for days. Finally the boys declared that the future of D. Kwon & Co. lay on the shoulders of my sister and me because Young Mahn would return to the mainland to his job and Young Chul had his church. For weeks Chung Hee and I wrestled with the terrible burden—too great for my sister with a husband and two little ones, and for me with my assignment as a new teacher.

The solution to the problem came unexpectedly and most dramatically one Saturday morning a few months after our father's death.

The shop had scheduled the installation of a large order of Poinciana Draperies for a home in Waianae, some thirty miles out of town. Ironically, the painter, who was supposed to accompany the men that day as part of the installation crew, reported late to work and the crew left without him.

Feeling embarrassed, the painter decided to spend the morning hours cleaning his workshop by scraping the thick, encrusted build-up of paint, something he had been planning to do but had not found the spare time.

He poured paint thinner generously over the surface of his work area and started to scrape the floor. After an hour he paused for a break. He lit a cigarette on his way out of the paint shop.

Before he knew it a roaring fire started behind him, and in no time the whole factory was engulfed in flames. The painter had forgotten to close the door behind him. Almost all the machinery and the stock went up in smoke or became waterlogged by the time the firemen arrived. This unbelievable disaster crushed any hopes and plans Chung Hee and I might have had for the business.

We spent weeks cleaning and sorting the salvageable items in the factory. After a long, arduous, and careful assessment of the damages and the situation, my sister and I reached the very difficult decision to close the shop permanently.

Informing the employees of this decision was painful. We had seen them engage in backbreaking labor to try to restore the shop to some semblance of order after the fire so that the business and their jobs could continue.

We gathered the employees together one morning to inform them of our decision. They stated they had guessed the end was imminent. They were sad but not bitter nor angry. On this last day we were together one of them said philosophically, "Now Mr. Kwon has the business he loved so much. He has taken it with him!"

Epilogue

MY father lies at peace beside my mother in the serenity of the memorial park. A profusion of flowers and green grass—which my mother loved so much—covers the landscape around them.

After our father's death, Young Mahn pursued a successful career as a certified public accountant. Young Chul continued in the ministry, much loved by his parishioners in the Congregational churches in Honolulu. Chung Hee earned a law degree and opened her own law office. And I was a high school English teacher until my retirement.

With hard work, great sacrifice, and ultimate joy my parents attained the dreams for the good life in their adopted land as well as a college education for each of their children. However, their cherished dream for the freedom of their country from their captors was only partially realized after a costly world war involving men, arms, and bombs; the northern half of their country, tragically, fell into the hands of communists.

My parents' inherent honesty, integrity, and goodness served them well. But their adherence to the hallowed Old World custom of filial piety drove my father into conflict in achieving the good life for his children. Both he and my mother believed in and spoke often of dividing any wealth they amassed equally among their four children. Ironically, my father thought he was offering the blueprint for success to his children by requesting, then demanding, their devotion to his wishes by carrying on his Poinciana business. Although things went awry, he did not fail them.

Glossary

abuji   father
Ai gu   oh my god!
ajusi   uncle
akma   devil
a-ni-o   no, not so
banchan   an assortment of vegetable, meat, and fish dishes served with a meal
bu uk   kitchen
chi-ma   long skirt, usually pleated and full
cho-gori   short jacket top worn over a skirt
do dong num   thief
dduk kuk   a broth with slices of white rice cake
furo   (Japanese) hot tub
geta   (Japanese) wooden clogs
halmuni   grandmother
harabuji   grandfather
holo holo   (Hawaiian) to go out for pleasure
hwal sogi   art of shooting with a bow and arrow; archery
ibul   a quilt, often covered with silk
jal-senggyut-suh   handsome, good-looking
jan-che   a feast served on special occasions such as weddings or birthdays
jhun   sliced meat, fish, or vegetable dipped in egg batter and fried
ji-rral   having a fit, crazy
juin   owner
kama   a palanquin, sedan chair

kan-jang   soy sauce

kye   a system of borrowing a large sum of money from a group
   of friends

kapakahi   (Hawaiian) crooked, uneven

kuh reh?   Is that so?

kuh reh!   That is so! True!

lau hala   (Hawaiian) plaited pandanus leaf

mal-lata   thin and scrawny

mang-hal-num   son-of-bitch, someone believed to be evil

Man sei!   Hurrah! Long live our country! Ten thousand years!

namul   a vegetable prepared with a sauce

nu-reh   sallow

nul-dwi-gi   see-saw jump

nu-reum-juk   skewered meats and vegetables on a stick

omoni   mother

sahng   dining table

sangchu ssam   lettuce wraps

sul   liquor made with rice

to shirak   lunch packed in a box

tubu   tofu (soybean curd)

u-mul   a well

weh-num   derisive word for the Japanese meaning "small guy,
   small in size"

yangban   gentleman, usually wealthy and well-educated

yi-min   a settler in a new land, immigrant

yobo   term of address of endearment to a spouse

Index

About the Author

Margaret K. Pai taught English at Kailua, Roosevelt, and Farrington high schools on Oahu. After her retirement, she began writing short Hawaiian legends, poems, and personal reminiscences. She has won prizes in local writing contests, and several of her pieces have been published. She presently lives and writes in Honolulu.

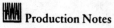 **Production Notes**

This book was designed by Roger Eggers.
Composition and paging were done on the
Quadex Composing System and typesetting on
the Compugraphic 8400 by the design and
production staff of University of Hawaii Press.

The text typeface is Sabon and the display
typeface is Gill Sans.

Offset presswork and binding were done by
Vail-Ballou Press, Inc. Text paper is Glatfelter
Offset Vellum, basis 50.

LaVergne, TN USA
11 December 2010
208305LV00001B/3/A